201 GARDEN SHRUBS IN COLOUR

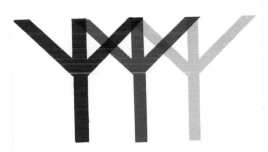

In the same series:

200 HOUSE PLANTS IN COLOUR *by G. Kromdijk*

FLOWER ARRANGEMENT WEEK BY WEEK *by Katinka Hendrichs*

First published in Great Britain in 1973

ISBN 0 7188 2044 4

Printed in the Netherlands

JAAP HAGE

201 GARDEN SHRUBS
IN COLOUR

Translated by Demy and Jaap Hage

LUTTERWORTH PRESS • GUILDFORD AND LONDON

CONTENTS

FOREWORD

Readers should not take the title of this book 201 SHRUBS IN COLOUR too literally, for not only does it describe considerably more than 201 plant species and varieties, but among them there are also conifers, roses climbing plants and those suitable for ground-cover.

The illustrations, mad and selected with utmost care, are intended to help gardening amateurs to identify plants which they may have seen growing in another garden, or to select those that appeal to them — for their flowers or their foliage or their shape, or suitable for a particular soil or size of garden or aspect.

Included in the text, in which I have often provided a note of the original home of the plant as well as the origin of its scientific name, is practical advice on planting, care, pruning and ideal position.

Attention has been given to pioneer plants which can be planted when a new garden is being made.

Separate sections deal with pruning and propagation and extensive lists and summaries give all manner of useful information.

A glance at a nursery catalogue, sometimes containing as many as 10,000 species and varieties, will convince readers of the impossibility, within such a book as this, of being anything but selective, however, I believe it will introduce many new plants and varieties to readers (and remind them of many others) and provide a great deal of information.

May this book, created in close co-operation with my wife, contribute to the pleasure derived by many people from their gardens and their gardening.

Jaap Hage

INTRODUCTION

When planning a new garden or making changes to an existing one, most careful consideration must be given to the future development of the plants. The descriptions in this book, therefore, tell you what you need to know about the distance you must allow between plants, for their ideal development above ground and to ensure that their roots will not hinder neighbouring plants.

Spacing

In a new garden plants should be given plenty of space at first. This will prevent the branches becoming crowded within a few years and allows them, and the surrounding plants, to get the maximum light. Only by that means will they live up to expectations. This applies even to grass, which will die without sufficient sunlight. A garden that will give pleasure for years should include shrubs of medium size. The smaller the garden, the greater the need for care in the planning. One often notices that small front gardens, planted a number of years ago, have a single shrub or a group that has become too dominating. It is perhaps still pleasant to look at and true to the beauty of leaves and flowers promised in the catalogue, but it crowds out other plants. Garden lovers should pull up dominating plants or do some hard pruning, though many gardeners seem to lack the courage this requires.

Position and soil

The position in the garden and the type of soil will greatly influence the choice of plants. The descriptions and lists at the back of this book will provide some guidance. Of course the conditions provided by a dry sandy soil are completely different from those on heavy clay. But you can help to change situations of this sort if you wish. For instance, some of the planting holes made in advance can be filled with peat moss that will widen the chances considerably, specially with rhododendrons and azaleas. Light and shade, wind and sunshine are also important factors, and in the descriptions, as well as in the summaries, attention is given to the needs of the plants in these respects.

If you are starting a garden from scratch it is a good idea to plant undemanding varieties at first. They ask little from the soil. Moreover they will prevent erosion of the top soil in the event of heavy rains and strong winds, especially on sloping land. The vegetation will improve the microclimate in the future garden; under protection of 'pioneer plants' a careful start can be made with the final planting scheme.

(Trans) planting with discretion

A favourable time for planting and transplanting is the months in which the plants are dormant, but it is obvious that snow covered ground will not receive the roots kindly. Deciduous plants indicate their dormant state very clearly. The best time to transplant evergreens is in October/November and March/April, provided the ground is not frozen hard. Planting in spring means that there is no longer serious danger of frost damage. Moreover the rising of the sap will stimulate root development.

Growing in containers, which is general practice in modern nurseries, has lengthened the planting time considerably. The roots can stay in the medium in which they are already growing, so the transplanting causes the minimum interference. Especially late in the season these plants should be watered well. The container, often made out of tarred paper or polythene, should be cut open and removed before planting, but the root balls should not be disturbed, other than unravelling the coiled roots at the sides.

The transplanting of conifers can be done from September, at any rate before snow and frost can be expected, or in April before the growth is starting again. They are always delivered with a root ball and this should not be broken up during planting, but the coiled roots must be spread out to provide a good anchorage for the tree. Thorough watering is always necessary.

A moist welcome

If shrubs and roses look somewhat dry on arrival they should be watered right away, even before planting. It might be necessary to put the roots into the water over-night, but if the plant has been delivered with a root ball or in a container the ball might disintegrate and that diminishes its survival chances considerably. Only azaleas and rhododendrons with root balls can stand a good bath.

7

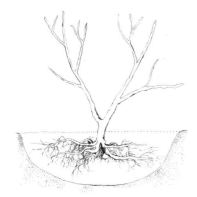

If plants cannot be planted immediately after their arrival because the ground is too hard or very wet, they should be firmly heeled in a protected place or kept in a cold garage or shed until conditions improve.

A wide berth

Planting holes, both in width and depth, should be about one-third larger than the size of the root system. Some fertile compost of garden loam can be put into the hole and, according to the circumstances, it can be watered in advance. The soil in the hole can be mixed with moist peat moss or compost, but in no case with fresh manure as this could harm the roots.

Broken, too long, or damaged roots should be cut off with a sharp knife and then the plant is placed into the hole in such a way that the roots are spread out horizontally; by shaking them gently it is possible to cover them with a thin layer of earth. Only after that is the planting hole filled and then the plant should be just as high above the soil as in its previous position. Only lilacs and Clematis can be planted a little deeper.

Finally the soil is trodden down carefully around the stem; in this way the centre will be somewhat deeper than the surrounding soil which will prevent the water given after planting from running away. If the weather is dry watering should be repeated several times. Mulching with peat moss, straw or dry leaves can prevent drying out of the soil around the plant.

Pruning

When transplanting there often will be a good opportunity to do some pruning. Weak shoots can be removed completely. If the plant flowers on one-year-old shoots, then strong branches can be cut back to a third, sometimes to half their length. Frost and drying out damage often indicates how much a branch should be pruned back. Shrubs transplanted in autumn are pruned only in spring. In all cases it is important that the top buds point outward; they conserve the right shape of the plant.

Winter pruning of established plants is appreciated by Cornus, Ceanothus, alder, Buddleia and several willow varieties, but will be disastrous to plants flowering on last year's or older branches, such as Magnolia, Prunus (flowering cherries), lilacs, and Hamamelis (witch hazel).

A well planned scheme

The tendency of the novice gardener is to go around the shrubs with a pruning knife or a pair of secateurs, cutting away branches at random, but this can have disastrous results. No pruning at all would be preferable, but undoubtedly a well planned pruning scheme will increase the beauty of most plants.

Rules can hardly be given but amateurs may learn by bitter experience. The purpose of pruning is to preserve the natural shape of the shrub and therefore some knowledge of the growing habits is necessary. The goal of pruning is also the removal of branches hampering the growth of others, and the eradication of branches too old to flower and dead wood in general. Nothing will flower in the dark centre of a plant; only from branches exposed to full light can flowers be expected. To improve a plant's condition we might prune some branches in late winter; it is often possible to get the trimmings to flower in water indoors; this goes for Forsythia, cherries, Hamamelis and Cydonia.

If necessary early flowering shrubs with their buds on the old wood might be pruned a little after flowering. Dead wood can be pruned earlier as it hampers buds and young shoots in their development. Thick, old and hardly flowering branches should be removed; the difference between dark old wood and light new shoots is usually obvious.

Healthy but leggy rhododendrons can be rejuvenated by hard pruning. Some old manure put around the base of the plant will promote the regrowth. With rhododendrons, azaleas and lilacs the dead flowers should be cut away as the development of seeds will delay the growth of new buds. The flowering in the next season depends on the development of the new shoots on which flower buds will be formed in autumn.

Plant descriptions often mention that pruning is not necessary, especially with conifers. That means that the natural attractive shape will only suffer under too industrious pruning. Most conifers, except those used for hedging, do not tolerate pruning. Only odd shoots spoiling the shape should be removed in summer, and in case a double top shoot develops the weaker one should be cut off.

POINTS TO CONSIDER
WHEN BUYING PLANTS

Novices in the garden world are inclined to worry about the quality of the plants offered and wonder what points should be considered when buying.

Generally one can rely on good nurseries and garden centres. Many garden lovers establish good relations with a gardener or a man with a market stall, who has supplied them satisfactorily for a long time. Mail-order houses, though there are many reliable firms among them, cannot always be trusted. Well-known firms that have been in business for many years are always better than firms which suddenly spring up and offer plants at reduced prices.

Deciduous shrubs should have three or more branches of three feet in length; the roots should be fine and reasonable moist. Of course a whole day in the sun at a market stall or in a garden centre diminishes the survival chances of a plant considerably. The branches should be rigid without any wrinkles in the bark. Spring flowering plants, such as lilacs and rhododendrons, should have clearly swollen terminal flower buds and in spring even nearly visible flowers. A good shrub has been pruned back once by the nurseryman, in order to promote the formation of branches. If the shrub is small and has apparently never been pruned back then it is inferior and would need another year in the nursery.

Evergreen plants should be delivered with a root ball or in a container. The leaves should be strong, have a good colour without holes caused by insects, and no spots or blotches, except of course with variegated plants. The leaves should be present low on the branches; leggy plants will stay that way. On the leaves, in particular on the underside, no scales of insects should be visible. A silvery shade and small webs on rhododendron leaves indicate the presence of Japanese flies, which are extremely hard to destroy. Leaves with holes can point to weevils in the root balls.

Conifers with bare brown patches will never show any regrowth in those places. Pyramidals, such as Chamaecyparis and Thuja, should not have any empty places in their foliage, spruces and firs no bare branches. Even small specimen of conifers should have the fine form that makes the full grown tree so attractive. A good conifer has a firm root ball with many thin white rootlets and in the nursery it should have been root pruned at sometime for shipment. An inspection for scale insects is necessary; Taxus in particular often has them in large numbers.

The foliage should be of the right colour and have a firm texture. Conifers that have been too dry and wilted have difficulty in recovering, if they ever do, and therefore especially the yellow varieties always need thorough watering after planting.

Climbing plants are delivered in containers and the quality depends on the quantity of roots present. Appearance is not always important. Clematis in particular can look very sick and yet still be capable of climbing to the roof within a short time.

PROPAGATION

Sooner or later many garden lovers want to propagate plants with their own hands and many even construct a frame or a small greenhouse for that purpose.

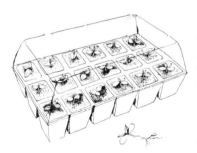

A complete manual for propagation would fill several books, but in a few lines some information can be given that might be useful. Experience has shown that a 'green thumb' Is a very important asset to the amateur gardener. Possessors of this useful limb seem to sense what is possible and what is not, but even they might find some help in a number of rules laid down by professionals.

Sowing is not the most obvious propagation method for the greater numbers of plants described in this book. Most of them are varieties and hybrids; their seed will seldom result in a plant with the same qualities as the parent plant. Therefore propagating by asexual means – without seed – is necessary. Some of these methods can be clarified as follows:

Hardwood cuttings are taken from dormant shoots. Mostly the lower section of old branches is too hard for this purpose and also lacks other qualities. The top of the branches is often too soft and not fully matured, but the middle section contains active tissue as well as reserve nutrients, both indispensable for growth.

To propagate simple shrubs, such as Weigela or Spiraea, one or two middle sections of a length of 8–10 inches can be taken. Pruning the shrubs on a frost-free day in November or December creates the right conditions for making cuttings. With a sharp knife a short cut is made right under a bud; the bark should not be damaged.

The cuttings can be tied in little bundles that are heeled in outside in dry soil for hibernation. In the meantime life within the cutting continues; on the wounds new tissue, called a 'callus', and even small rootlets will appear.

In March or April the cuttings are dug up carefully; the tender roots must not be damaged. Then they are set out in their permanent place. Many species of Cotoneaster, Buddleia, Deutzia, Forsythia, Kerria, Lonicera tatarica, Potentilla (take strong branches), roses, Salix (very large cuttings), Sambucus, Spiraea, Tamarix pentandra and Weigela can be propagated by this simple method.

Softwood cuttings are made from young shoots not yet hardened into wood, but firm enough to be inserted in the medium — a mixture of sand and peat moss. This should be done immediately after cutting the shoots; a wilted cutting will usually not take.

If cuttings are placed under glass the frame should be protected against fierce sunlight. If they are covered by plastic sheets the condensation usually gives sufficient protection against the sun.

Softwood cuttings should preferably be cut in the morning. The cuttings are placed between sheets of slightly moist paper to prevent drying out. Clematis, Japanese azaleas and climbing Lonicera varieties are very suitable species to which to apply this method. Provided the terminal buds are closed it is possible to make softwood cuttings of Ilex, Cotinus and Picea. Completely matured shoots can be taken from Taxus,

Chamaecyparis, Juniperus, Mahonia, Aucuba and Prunus laurocerasus later in the season.

The base of the cuttings can be dipped in hormone rooting powder to assist the formation of roots.

Division is often possible with shrubs that come out of the ground with more than one shoot or form strong off-shoots or runners, such as Erica, Pachysandra, Kerria and many others; their habits are mentioned in the section on individual plant descriptions.

To make a division, part of the plant, with one or more shoots, is freed from soil and cut off. Small plants, such as Pachysandra and Erica, are temporarily taken out of the soil completely and then divided into pieces; all of them can be planted out again. A close inspection of the plant before cutting is obviously recommended.

Layering is an old method demanding little care, but a good knowledge of the plant and its possibilities are indispensable, e.g. Cornus, a shrub very hard to propagate in any other way, is very suitable for layering. Furthermore Corylopsis, Juniperus varieties, Thuja, Magnolia, and even Azalea and Rhododendron, can be propagated in this interesting way.

The method has been adopted by nature as one may see when a low branch touches the soil, often forming roots and starting a life of its own. As a consequence, plants with low growing branches are very suitable for layering. The shoots should not be too old and rigid, nor too young and too tender.

In summer, when the branches are still flexible, they should be carefully bent to the ground that has been loosened and enriched with a little compost or peat moss. The curved section is anchored to the ground with a peg or a piece of bent wire. Afterwards everything is covered with soil and pressed down carefully. Moreover the top part of the shoot can be tied to a stake that keeps it upright.

It might take a long time, even two years, before the layers have sufficient roots, and so are ready to stand on their own feet. Then the connection between the motherplant and the layer is cut; in the next planting season the rooted layer can be planted in another place.

Layering is an effective form of propagating and many an amateur will see it as a challenge, to try it out himself. In some nurseries motherplants may be seen, surrounded by a lot of young plants, but in an amateur's garden there will be hardly place for such a family.

Grafting, finally, is a method demanding certain professional skill, but in view of the results achieved by amateurs with a green thumb a short item on it is certainly justified.

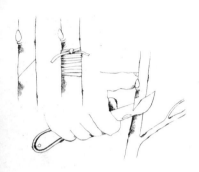

A complete description would go beyond the scope of this book, but the principle is that the plant to be propagated is brought into contact with the understock or roots of a related, possibly wild, form, sometimes even an imported one. Generally speaking, one needs a frame or greenhouse for grafting, except when it is done with a dormant 'eye' and in summer, such as with roses.

On a rooted understock the scion — of a better or different form — is placed, but at first both parts must be cut with a sharp knife. The two cuts should fit perfectly and to keep them together the help of a rubber band, raffia or string is indispensable. If everything goes well callus tissue will make a connection and a new, more noble plant is born.

The application of this method demands some know-how; skill, and lessons from a professional, are very useful.

SCIENTIFIC NAMES

Writers of books about plants are often reproached with the remark that the scientific plant names are so complicated. Indeed, in the plant lists one may find names nearly unpronounceable and, on first sight, incomprehensible too. If the plant has an English name it will be mentioned in this book, but often exotic plants lack an acceptable national name.

Still the scientific names, seeming so complicated, are built very logically; they are indispensable to the international trade and to scientific communication.

As a matter of fact, industry envy the botanical world for the international system that does not exist in other circles. Once the official name is mentioned, nurserymen and botanical experts coming together from all countries know what one is talking about.

Folk or popular names are different and useless in international conversation. We owe the scientific system to the Swedish botanist Linnaeus.

The names are built up according to a fixed pattern. Always the name of the genus comes first; it is invariably written with a capital letter. Then comes the name of the species, nowadays with a small letter, and next comes the name of the variety. In accordance with the latest practice the latter is written with an initial capital letter and placed between inverted commas.

A complete book could be written about the origin of plant names. Often they are very old; some of them are latinised folk names, others commemorate well-known botanists who found the first specimen or described it. The names of plants hybridised with each other may be used, like Mahoberberis for a hybrid between Mahonia and Berberis. Often, too, real or supposed qualities are recorded in the name, e.g. 'alba' stands for white, 'praecox' for early, 'monogyna' for single stigma. They can also remind one of the origin of the plant, such as 'atlantica', 'siberica' and 'maritima'.

Sometimes the genus name under which the plant was known in the past, but proved to be wrong or no longer suits the plant, is placed in the second position. An example is the word 'aquifolium'; in olden times that name was given to all plants with thorny leaves. Similarly other plants can be described with additions such as 'salicifolia (-us or -um)' indicating that the leaves remind us of the willow (Salix). 'Ilicifolia' points to characteristics of holly (Ilex) and 'liliflora' is an indication that the flower looks more or less like a lily.

Often latinised Christian or proper names commemorate the discoverers of the plants. 'Carlesii' and 'Hugonis' remind us of the missionaries Carlos and Hugo who found the plants. 'Sieboldii', 'thunbergii' and 'kaempferi' commemorate surgeons on ships of the East Indian Company who found original plants in the Far East and brought many new varieties to Western countries.

The names of varieties often take care of a still finer distinction; they mention properties indicating how they differ from other members of the plant family, e.g. 'Pyramidalis Compacta' means conical shaped and compact growing, 'Grandiflora (-us, -um)' indicates large flowering. Plants with many varieties (cultivars), such as roses and rhododendrons, often bear names given by the originator to commemorate certain events or somebody famous at that time, such as with Rhododendron 'Winston Churchill' or the old rose 'Edith Cavell'. There are hundreds of varieties with a proper name; often the plant is remembered longer than the person that originally inspired the grower. Sometimes there is a certain system in names: a series of well-known Japanese azaleas were given the names of famous composers.

Very complicated is the rule prescribing that the oldest name is the valid one. Anyone who is able to prove that a certain plant has been described earlier by another person can have this recorded and it can be changed accordingly. Many plants have had three or even four names in their life.

New botanical systems sometimes change the plant names. Officially the name Azalea does not exist any-more, this group being absorbed by the genus Rhododendron. For practical reasons in this book, and in many others, the original name has been maintained.

The amateur gardener, too, will do well to use the official names when ordering plants; in this way he speaks the language of the plant world. The nurseryman thus knows, or at least should know, his intentions right away. Asking for Chamaecyparis obtusa 'Nana Gracilis' will indicate the exact conifer at once, but asking for a prostrate dwarf Hinoki cypress might mean searching for a long time.

In this book both the scientific and the common name (if any) are given. The latest official names, apart from Azalea, are used together with the most recent spelling.

Abies nordmanniana

Young cones of Abies nordmannia

ABIES (Silver fir)

Among the conifers, the silver firs occupy an important place. In general appearance the difference between Abies and Picea is not large and therefore the two genera are often confused. Still there are some characteristic differences: the cones of abies grow upright on one-year-old shoots and are shed in autumn, leaving only a woody spike. Picea cones are pendulous and fall off completely. In the cases where there are no cones the leaves show the difference: if a picea leaf is torn off a small piece of bark will come with it, but with an abies leaf the bark and the base cushion stay unharmed.

A. nordmanniana is a strong growing cylindrical tree that reaches up to 45 feet and achieves a wide spread of 15 feet within a few years. Therefore it is not suitable for small gardens, but as a solitary tree it will be very decorative. The leaves are dark green and the branches grow close to the ground, so nothing will grow at the base of the tree.

A. procera 'Glauca' is sometimes mistaken for a blue spruce on account of the blue colour of the young shoots. It is a silvery blue form of the species that originated from California. Not being a fast grower, this blue 'noble fir' can still make a sizeable tree, bearing beautiful cones of a length of over 8 inches at an early age; these drop in autumn. The cones only develop if the tree is protected against cold winds.

To keep it to a pleasant shape pruning may be necessary. It is essential to maintain one single leading shoot. If competing shoots appear they should be removed from the main axis with a sharp knife. If the tree grows to one side the shoots there should be pruned a little. Propagation of the varieties is by grafting on an understock of common Abies.

17

Acer palmatum 'Atropurpureum'   *A. p. 'Dissectum'*

ACER (Maple)

There are about two hundred species, not to speak of the large number of varieties. All leaf shapes are represented; some of them not only have a nice colour in spring and summer, but also attain beautiful autumn shades.

A fine form of the green-leaved A. palmatum is the variety 'Atropurpureum' shown above. Its thin overhanging shoots bear seven-lobed leaves that can be damaged by late night frosts and bleak spring winds. At the end of the summer these leaves are apt to fade, but later they present brilliant autumn colouring. The shrub can be as wide as it is high and takes several years to reach a height of 10 feet. Planted in front of a group of dark evergreen conifers or a light wall, this maple will provide a fine contrasting effect.

Still slower is the growth of the other variety shown in the picture above. A. palmatum 'Dissectum', it is a rather low dwarf shrub, very suitable for rock gardens. The fine deeply cut leaves and the shoots growing in all directions make it very suitable for displays at spring flower shows, as also is A. palmatum 'Dissectum Atropurpureum' with its bronze red leaves. Very attractive is the yellowish Japanese maple A. japonicum 'Aureum' but the fine golden leaves are easily damaged by hot sun and strong winds.

All varieties enjoy a moist soil with a lot of humus. Though the leaves look their best in direct sunshine a slightly shaded position will prevent burning of the leaves. As a matter of fact A. palmatum 'Atropurpureum' will not achieve its reddist colouring in full sun.

Maples need no pruning; only dead branches can be removed. Propagation is by grafting, sometimes also by layering.

Acer negundo 'Argenteomarginatum'   *Acer dissectum 'Atropurpureum'*

ACER (Maple)

Owners of not too large a garden often search for a tree that will not dominate every-thing within a short time. As felling trees is – often rightly – considered a crime nowadays, and as one gets attached to the layout of a garden, it may happen that a small weeping willow becomes a veritable tyrant in ten years' time or even less, preventing all other plants and even grass from growing.

On this point A. negundo is a modest grower, and the variegated varieties 'Variegatum' and 'Aureomarginatum' are favourites. The green ones are less attractive and often grow too fast, but all of them are hardy and will survive, provided their position is not too exposed, even in more or less polluted air.

The leaves of 'Variegatum' have golden blotches that will not fade in strong sunshine and give the necessary contrasting effect in the garden. The green winter bark is also decorative. The finest variety is 'Aureomarginatum' with golden edges on the leaves as the name implies. The bright green shoots and the light edges on the feathery pale to mid green leaves, with five to seven leaflets, contrast very well with dark conifers and in autumn with the reddish shades of other deciduous trees and shrubs.

These maples are strong and hardy, withstand sun and shadow and, moreover, thrive in many types of soil. Green shoots or suckers on the roots of variegated varieties should be pruned heavily as otherwise they will dominate the variegated ones pretty soon. Other pruning is not required.

Propagation of variegated forms is by grafting on seedlings of the green ones.

19

Aesculus parviflora

AESCULUS PARVIFLORA (Autumn horse chestnut)

To most people a chestnut is a mighty tree with a broad crown, admired in parks or in large squares and therefore this shrub-like variety comes as a surprise. It is not only suitable for a medium sized garden, but moreover it is valuable on account of its flowering time, between June and August, when the glorious period of other trees and shrubs, and certainly of the chestnuts, is already over. At that time this shrub is covered with erect panicles of white flowers with yellow blotches of a length of 8–12 inches, hardly smaller than those of the other chestnuts. On closer inspection the flowers seem somewhat smaller, but the long pink stamens give them a special character. The leaves are smooth and mid-green, often turning beautiful autumn colours later and are of a size of about 8 inches.

This plant originates from the southern States of North America and can reach a size of about 6–7 feet eventually. Its long suckers in the ground grow out in all directions.

This chestnut will do well in any soil; the shadow of larger trees does not hamper the growth very much. In the middle of a lawn Aesculus parviflora can have a very decorative function.

The natural form being very attractive, pruning means only removing old branches.

Propagation is simple, as pruned suckers can be used and layering is very easy. Branches touching the ground will root without difficulty.

Ailanthus altissima

AILANTHUS ALTISSIMA (Tree of heaven)

A modern house surrounded by a lawn might look well with a decorative plant, adapted to the style and to the surrounding landscape. In such cases there might be room for a fast growing, somewhat exotic, tree such as Ailanthus altissima, the tree of heaven.

Coming into leaf very late in the season, this tree will not take the sunlight from spring flowers. Later on the thick stems have green, pinnate leaves, 12–30 inches long and composed of fifteen to thirty leaflets; on new shoots they can be still longer. Large greenish orange flowers stand in terminal panicles.

The nature of the tree is to grow fast and high. If the garden is too small for a sizeable tree it can be cut annually in February to about 20 inches from the base to keep it compact.

The tree will send out many root suckers that can be used for propagation.

As a matter of fact, a tree of heaven tolerates air pollution. In New York it is generally used as a street tree, though the branches are rather brittle for that purpose.

The tree of heaven is satisfied with any soil, even under poor circumstances where other vegetation is hardly possible. It can be used as a pioneer plant and forerunner of the final planting; the fast growth gives an immediate protection.

In its country of origin, China, a natural height of about 90 feet can be reached (hence its name which is derived from *ailanto*, a word signifying a tree tall enough to reach the skies) but this can hardly be expected in this part of the world.

Amelanchier f. villosa (A. canadensis)

AMELANCHIER CANADENSIS (June berry)

A plant with many possibilities in the garden, as well as providing undergrowth in woodlands. It will do very well in town gardens on account of its great tolerance of air pollution.

In April the tree is completely covered by small white flowers in clusters. The young shoots, coming after the flowers, also display beautiful colours just like the leaves — first silvery haired, later bronze, in summer bright green and afterwards of beautiful autumn shades. Finally the reddish purple, almost black, fruit make the June berry a real all-purpose plant. The dense shrub can grow up to about 30 feet. The early flowers attract many bees, as there is not much pollen to be found elsewhere in the garden and their visits lead to the small fruits that are sweet, juicy and edible to the birds.

The June berry is not demanding as far as soil goes; it will grow more or less everywhere. Pruning is not necessary and propagation is possible by means of seeds, but layering too is practicable; lower branches, bent to the soil, will root within a year.

Aralia elata

ARALIA ELATA (Japanese Angelica Tree)

This remarkable tree originates from Manchuria, which is indicated by its former scientific name Dimorphantus mandschurica.

In winter as well as in summer the angelica tree has a characteristic appearance. In winter especially the thick light coloured stem, covered with numerous short thorns, gives a special character to the plant. Its stem can be 9–15 feet high. In summer bipinnate, sometimes even tripinnate, leaves can have a diameter of 30 inches and even more, which contrasts with the appearance of the tree in winter, when it is thin and slender.

The tree looks particularly fine in the month of August when there are few shrubs in flower. The angelica tree will be covered then by large yellowish-white panicles, consisting of tiny flowers that need close inspection to show their graceful form.

The growth of many underground suckers can be an advantage as well as a disadvantage. Garden lovers wanting to surprise their friends with an exotic plant can make use of the suckers : they can cut them off and use them for replanting. People with smaller gardens, not wanting a manchurian wood, can cut off the suckers completely with roots and stems and thus keep the plant to a reasonable size.

The aralia is best at home in stony dry soil. Propagation is made easy by the suckers, but the variety with white edged leaves, 'Variegata', and the one with golden leaves, 'Aureovariegata', can only be propagated by difficult grafting on stems of the green form and therefore professional skill is needed.

23

Aristolochia durior

ARISTOLOCHIA DURIOR (Dutchman's pipe)

This book gives some attention to climbing plants, as they provide a vertical dimension to the garden, an aspect important in itself. Furthermore they not only increase the extent of leaves and flowers, but can be a great help by providing colour and texture and a feature of interest to less attractive houses or out-buildings. Even a modern bungalow may need some flippant elements but, in general, old farms or country houses can be beautified in this way. Leaves, and eventually flowers, growing around the windows give a friendly character to any home.

A less well-known plant with great summer possibilities is Aristolochia durior, native of the southern United States, but now well established in Western Europe.

The name Dutchmans' pipe is derived from the yellow, brown and green flowers, shaped like an old-fashioned Dutch tobacco pipe. In colder areas the plant does not bloom very prolificly, but still the main attraction lies in the large heart-shaped leaves, often 15 inches in diameter and laid out in a regular pattern like roofing tiles that look very attractive against any wall.

On good soil — with some clay for preference — the plant quickly grows to about 30 feet and covers a large area, especially in a sunny situation, within a short time. Pruning can be limited to cutting back some of the very vigorous shoots. Propagation is possible by layering or cuttings.

Aucuba japonica 'Variegata'

AUCUBA

At the end of the eighteenth century aucubas came to Europe from Japan – the name comes from the Japanese name *Aokiba*. Unfortunately, they became overplanted and formed the foundation of many Victorian shrubberries. They proved, however, to be remarkably tolerant to polluted air. The shrubs, keeping their smooth laurel-like leaves in winter, have an attractive natural shape.

Aucubas are unisexual ; only female plants have inconspicuous flowers, later followed by bright, scarlet, ovoid berries. People wanting berries should plant one male plant among six females. It is remarkable that in the past male and female plants were known under different names.

A. japonica 'Variegata', shown above, has attractive variegated leaves. There is a somewhat less hardy variety 'Crotonifolia' ; the other varieties are hardly known.

The plant will thrive in any soil and in any situation ; it grows in the sun as well as in the shade. It is one of only few evergreen shrubs doing well under large trees and in shady yards, and even resists constant dripping from above. It can be used in urns and other containers and even survives indoors for a short time.

A. mollis

Azalea pontica 'Coccinea Speciosa'

AZALEA

Here the nomenclature presents a problem, because officially ·all azaleas belong to the botanical genus Rhododendron, so theoretically there are no azaleas anymore. Still these plants are so well known under their original name they are included here.

Both azaleas pictured above belong to the deciduous type. They are the results of intensive hybridisation and, as a consequence, have lost many of their original characteristics. They are descendants of the yellow Rhododendron luteum, native to the Balkans and Asia Minor. In the Belgian nursery centre, Ghent, they were crossed with American varieties for the first time and this resulted in the well-known Ghent or Pontica azaleas. On good soil with humus and no lime they will grow to about 7 feet and flower in soft pastel colours from yellow to red around the middle of May.

Still larger is the variation in the mollis hybrids, descendants of yellow Rhododendron molle, originating in China. To achieve best results they should be planted in groups and in lime-free soil with humus, where they can reach 5 feet within a short time. As they are liable to get somewhat leggy a group of lower plants at the base will enhance the beauty. Pruning should be done with utmost care as older branches are liable to die prematurely, which reduces flowering.

Seedlings can be bought to colour, selected in red, orange and yellow hybrids; moreover there are named varieties in shades between yellow and orange-red. The best time to make a choice is shortly before flowering, when the buds already show some colour and transplanting is still possible. Propagation is by cuttings and grafts.

26

Knap Hill azalea 'Harvest Moon'   *Mixed group of A. mollis and A. japonica*

AZALEA

The Knaphill and Exbury azaleas are a hardy, comparatively modern group of colourful deciduous varieties. They were bred originally by Mr. Anthony Waterer at the Knap Hill Nursery, near Woking, Surrey, and further improved at the Exbury Estate in Hampshire by the late Lionel de Rothschild.

Many have done so well that they have received awards after trial at the Royal Horticultural Society's Garden at Wisley in Surrey. Some that can be recommended are: 'Homebush', carmine-red and having an Award of Garden Merit; 'Strawberry Ice', Award of Garden Merit; 'Persil', pure white with golden-yellow blotch; 'Balzac', deep orange-red. These azaleas will grow well in full sun, provided the soil is well enriched with peat to hold moisture.

Azalea japonica

AZALEA

The evergreen Rhododendron obtusum is one of the many species that has given rise to the Japanese azaleas. Many hybrids have come from Japan, particularly the well-known Kurume azaleas which are reminiscent of Azalea indica, the tender kind which is sold by the thousands in pots during the winter for indoor decoration.

Very suitable for the small garden are the low growing 'Vuyk's Rosy-red' and 'Vuyk's Scarlet'. A. 'Amoenum', growing to 20 inches and of a spreading habit with small purple flowers, also does well in the rock garden. A taller plant with larger white flowers is the hardy variety 'Palestrina'.

As members of the heather family, these azaleas need liberal quantities of peat or leaf mould in a limeless soil. They grow best in half-shade but can stand full sun. Pruning should be limited to removing old and dead branches. In case of a long, dry winter a light cover with branches might prevent damage to the buds. When the buds are kept moist Japanese azaleas can be forced into flower early indoors from about Christmas. Plants can be propagated by half-ripe cuttings.

Recommended Japanese azaleas: 'Favorite' (deep pink), 'Hinodegini' (deep carmine red), 'John Cairns' (red), 'Orange Beauty' (soft orange), 'Beethoven' (large lilac flowers), 'Fedora' (deep pink), 'Kathleen' (dark pink), and 'Hinomayo' (pink).

Flowering times vary and can run from mid-April — early varieties in sheltered places — until the end of May.

Berberis buxifolia 'Nana'   *Berberis julianae*   *Berberis stenophylla*

BERBERIS (Barberry)

Evergreen barberry varieties are, on account of their different habits, important plants, often very suitable for small and rock gardens. They usually have fine leaves and, in addition, they produce brightly-coloured berries, making their appearance still more striking.

In spring, long before the full flowering season starts, the fragrant yellow flowers appear in great numbers, but in spite of their almost year-around programme of attractions barberries ask little attention and do not crowd themselves out of the garden in a short time. They can be combined with heather and bulbous plants, and as they do not need much sunlight they can be combined with Pachysandra, Skimmia or Hedera, growing under trees.

The first shrub pictured above is from Chile; its name is B. buxifolia 'Nana'. Those who wish to use shrubs for border edging, but find boxwood a little dull, have a colourful substitute in this barberry. The small shrubs, not reaching more than 20 inches, stand pruning very well; the fine foliage is tinted reddish brown in winter. Though they are very hardy they may drop their leaves in exposed places, but these come back in the following spring. Another species is B. julianae that came to Europe from Western China. This plant can reach 6–7 feet, the shiny, dark green leaves have sharp thorns along the edges. A lot of yellow flowers appear in May–June, followed by dark blue berries with a waxy bloom. The shrub can be used for an impenetrable hedge, is very hardy and does not object to exposed positions. Any soil and place will be suitable. Propagation by cuttings.

Berberis julianae   *Berberis x ottawensis 'Superba'*

BERBERIS (Barberry)

Besides the evergreen barberries, there are also deciduous types such as B. thunbergii, a native of Japan but now a well-known ornamental shrub all over the world.

B. thunbergii is, by its compact sturdy growth and its sharp spines, very suitable for hedges. The flowers are light yellow, the berries coral red, small and ovoid; the autumn shades of the green species are orange and flaming red. A short time is needed for a B. thunbergii hedge to get established; plant 12–15 inches apart.

Out of many hybrids a number of very attractive varieties have been selected, like 'Atropurpurea' with rich purple-red leaves and 'Atropurpurea Nana', a dwarf plant, very suitable for low edges. A green upright variety is 'Erecta', and very effective for edges is the new variety 'Rose Glow' with irregularly variegated leaves in pink and white, giving the impression that the plant is always in full flower. This variety is slow growing and worth buying.

A strong grower is B. ottawensis 'Superba' (above right) with dark brown shoots and branches that easily reach 7 feet. The large leaves are red with a slight white waxy bloom, the flowers are bright green, the berries bright red. A shrub can be used as a single specimen but also as part of a strong hedge; it is very hardy. Of the same size is the ever-green B. stenophylla (above left) with beautiful arching branches and orange-yellow flowers in May. Suitable for hedges and as a solitary specimen plant.

Barberries do not like lime in the soil. Deciduous varieties can be multiplied by seeds, the others by cuttings.

Buddleia davidii 'Royal Red'

Buddleia davidii 'Fascination'

BUDDLEIA DAVIDII (Butterfly bush)

Buddleias grow wild in North Asia, South America and South Africa. Their name commemorates the Rev. Adam Buddle, a vicar of Farnbridge in Essex.

When in early summer the flowering of many shrubs is declining the butterfly bush attracts numerous butterflies and bees that even manage to search out the honey scented flowers in the centre of a city. Many kinds of insects can be found drinking the nectar which seems to have such an intoxicating influence that they are undisturbed even when people approach.

The original butterfly bushes only had a short flowering period, but by hybridizing and selecting this has been extended so much that it now comprises half the summer. There are varieties in all kinds of colours : 'Fascination' has long pink plumes, 'Ile de France', branching strongly, flowers in a deep purple shade, 'White Cloud', has long clusters of pure white flowers. The pictured 'Royal Red', has relatively short but rich red-purple clusters, and the late variety 'Cardinal' is purple-red and long lasting.

Old, no longer attractive flowers should be cut away to make room for new shoots. In this way it is possible to extend the flowering period well into October.

Buddleias grow in any soil, but like the sunshine that encourages the visits of the butterflies. In cold winters the plants can suffer frost damage but at any rate the branches should be cut back to 8 inches from the ground in spring. Weak twigs should be removed completely. Propagation is by hardwood cuttings.

Buxus sempervirens

BUXUS SEMPERVIRENS (Common box)

The box is one of the oldest garden plants. Though native to the Mediterranean countries it has unfolded its small leathery, glossy dark green leaves in gardens all over the world for centuries.

Box is an early favourite because it is an evergreen and, moreover, can be cut in any desired shape, while its growth can be limited to any height which was especially appreciated by gardeners in olden times. With the right use of pruning shears it is possible to give the box all kinds of shapes, such as pyramids, spirals, chickens and bears, but this topiary art is becoming a lost craft nowadays.

As true evergreen, Buxus will always hold its own and as a consequence of the return to old styles and romantic gardens, in fashion now, it is experiencing a renaissance, as are also old garden statues and ornaments that can be surrounded by box spirals and pyramids.

There are also colourful varieties like 'Aureovariegata', with golden speckled leaves, and 'Marginata' with a golden edge. Buxus s. 'Suffruticosa' is a dwarf very suitable for edging that can be propagated by earthing up the plants and cutting off the rooted branches after a year. Other varieties can be propagated by cuttings. The soil is never a problem.

32

Callicarpa bodinierii var. giraldii

CALLICARPA

This remarkable berried shrub has no popular name, but it could be characterised as china berry as on this plant the round violet-purple berries, looking more like china beads than vegetable matter, are most striking. They appear in late summer and stay on till winter comes. The berries remain on the branches for a long time provided birds leave them alone. The name is derived from the Greek *kallos*, beautiful, and *karpos*, a fruit, in allusion to the berries.

In summer Callicarpa bodinieri 'Giraldii' is very inconspicuous, the narrow pale green leaves not being elegant and the small purple flowers being hidden by the foliage. The glorious period starts later: the foliage that first turns to autumn colours drops off early and then the berries become visible. This process can be speeded up by plucking off the leaves.

During winter and in colder areas the shrub can suffer some frost damage and therefore should be grown in a somewhat sheltered place; a sunny position against a southern wall is ideal. To promote the formation of many berries one should plant several shrubs together as cross pollination promotes fruiting. Any garden soil is acceptable.

Pruning can be limited to removing the old wood, in order to promote the growth of young shoots.

Propagation by seed generally gives inferior plants. Cuttings will show better results. A new variety 'Profusion' has more and larger berries; in the long run it will take the place of older varieties.

Calluna vulgaris 'H. E. Beale'   *C. v. 'Alportii'*

CALLUNA (Ling, heather)

Heather is at home in Western Europe and a good observer will soon discover that even in the field many forms deviate from the original species in flowers and leaves, as well as in colour and habit. After careful selection nurserymen have introduced many fine garden varieties; in particular the English firm Maxwell and Beale is very well-known in this field.

In the right soils all Calluna varieties can be planted irregularly over the ground and thus form a heather garden, together with the Erica varieties described elsewhere in this book. A careful selection of varieties makes it possible for callunas to be flowering in the garden from July until November. Even after that period many of them still have a function, especially the varieties with golden foliage such as 'Gold Haze' and variegated forms that will cheer up the garden during winter. Between rocks and paving stones cushion-forming varieties can be used.

As plants callunas are not very demanding, but they will grow best in soil with humus, but without lime. They are not suitable for wet or ill-drained land. They stand shade and full sun; plants that grow somewhat leggy and bare can be hard-pruned back in spring.

Some recommended varieties are C. vulgaris 'Alba Elata' (white), 'Gold Haze' (white with golden foliage), 'H. E. Beale' (double lilac pink flowers), 'Mullion' (deep pink – very low growing), 'Robert Chapman' (purple flowers and bronze leaves), 'Alportii' (purple-but without lime. They are not suitable for wet or ill-drained land. They stand shade and red). Propagation is by divisions and cuttings.

Campsis radicans

CAMPSIS RADICANS (Trumpet vine)

This came to us from the South Eastern United States and to flower well it needs a warm sunny position. In cold areas and in exposed positions it needs a light winter cover for some years. In the beginning the vines are not self-clinging and therefore a support is very welcome. After a few years the plant will be completely self supporting and in fertile soil a luscious growth may be expected. As a matter of fact the trumpet vine is very suitable to cover an unsightly wall or building.

In particular in a southern position, and in a somewhat protected place, the plant will become a tropical beauty. The charming ,sometimes more than 4 inches long, trumpet-shaped flowers are generally orange. The variety 'Madame Galen' a hybrid with another campsis, is the most showy and in a sheltered position the flowering period can be extended from July to the end of September.

In order to stimulate new shoots at the base the vine should be cut back to about 6 feet in the first year. Older plants should be pruned back every spring. The right place is a little above the spot where the new growth has started in the previous year. The flowers will appear on the young shoots.

With some varieties propagation of root cuttings is possible; hybrids can be grafted on understock.

Caragana arborescens 'Lorbergii'

CARAGANA ARBORESCENS (Pea tree) *Peashrub*

Pea trees originate from the Asian steppes where in extremely low temperatures winter storms are very dry. Therefore this shrub will not give any trouble even in most exposed places in cold areas. They grow to a little over man-size, and are suitable for backgrounds and hedges. They may also be used as pioneer plants even in poor sandy soil where they can pave the way for more sophisticated plantings after some time.

Like all Leguminosae, Caragana has the property to form nitrogen in its small root modules and can improve the soil in this way. The small yellow butterfly flowers appear in May, and though the shrub will flower even against a northern wall, they will be more numerous in a sunny position. At any rate the flowers are shortlived; later the small brown pods appear which gave the plant its name.

The erect growing forms include the variety 'Lorbergii', pictured above, with fern-like, pinnate leaves on arching branches, a very graceful plant. In other respects it is similar to C. arborescens. Sometimes the weeping variety 'Pendula' is grafted on a single stem of C. aborescens and a graceful weeping tree is the result. The species C. maximowicziana has long reddish brown shoots, covered with long thorns and large solitary flowers, yellow as well. C. aurantiaca remains very low growing and becomes broad; it is therefore suitable to cover dry sunny slopes.

Caraganas, seldom having any diseases, can be propagated by seeds and grafting. Pruning will only be necessary when shoots have become too long or when the plant's centre gets crowded.

Caenothus 'Gloire de Versailles'

CEANOTHUS (Californian lilac)

This plant deserves more attention on account of its attractive late summer flowering at a time that other plants are already past their prime. Under cold conditions a Californian lilac is liable to winter damage. In northern regions a little winter cover over the branches and the base might be useful. Should branches show frost damage, they can be pruned to the living wood and within a short time the new shoots will appear on which the beautiful flowers, looking more or less like miniature lilacs, will appear from July until October, sometimes even longer depending on the weather.

The best known varieties are hybrids between different species. Very attractive are 'Gloire de Versailles' (blue), 'Henri Desfossé' (purple-blue), 'Indigo', as the name implies indigo, pink 'Marie Simon', carmine-rose 'Perle Rose', and soft blue 'Topaz'.

The shrub will not grow higher than about 3 feet and therefore can be used as a low hedge or in a flower border. The soil should have a good humus content and be porous without lime.

In general the shrub is delivered in a pot ; during planting the root ball should be handled with care.

If possible plant the shrub against a south-facing wall and there it will seldom be damaged by cold.

Propagation is possible by layering and cuttings, also by sowing seed, but then named varieties will not come true to colour.

Cedrus atlantica 'Glauca'

CEDRUS ATLANTICA 'GLAUCA' (Blue Atlas cedar)

To many people the name of this tree has an appealing sound as the cedars of the Lebanon are mentioned in the Bible.

Cedars are hardly suitable for small gardens. The beautiful horizontal branches make them very conspicious trees that have been cultivated in the milder areas of Western Europe for several centuries.

The illustrated variety, C. atlantica 'Glauca', comes, as the name implies, from the Atlas mountains; it has been cultivated in Western Europe for about half a century. Still in that comparitively short time it has been distributed widely.

Its fast growth can be embarassing in small gardens, but this characteristic makes the cedar almost ideal planted in the centre of a spacious lawn, where in full sun the branches at the base will not die away -- a special attraction of this tree.

A cedar, provided the root ball be kept intact, will grow in any reasonably fertile soil, in particular if some old manure is used when planting. At the start a strong stake tied to the main stem may be useful; it will help to promote a vertical growth. Later the tree will stand on its own very well, even if it has to endure a lot of wind.

The most frequently planted variety is C. a. 'Glauca', with its hazy blue colour as the name implies, and, moreover, silvery young shoots in spring. In the first years it should not be pruned much.

Well-known forms are C. a. 'Aurea' with golden foliage, and the more upright growing C. a. 'Fastigiata', which is preferable for smaller gardens.

Cedrus deodara

CEDRUS DEODARA (Deodar)

This is one of the most important trees of the Himalaya mountains, where it reaches a height of about 200 feet, which must not be expected in Western Europe. Still this is a conifer, reminding one of far away countries. Its branches arch gracefully, yet without giving it the appearance of a weeping tree. The leaves are blue-grey when young and mature to dark green. The deodar looks its best when a centre branch is kept to create a real tree form.

Cedrus deodara is available in several varieties, such as the slow growing 'Aurea', more suitable for smaller gardens and with golden yellow shoots, later turning greenish yellow. This special colour makes the variety ideal for a garden lit by floodlight in winter. C. deodara 'Verticillata Glauca' has a more erect growth and larger blue-green leaves.

Pruning should be limited to keeping the tree in the right shape. If it is still young one should decide if a spreading or more erect shape is wanted. At any rate one centre branch should be allowed to grow up in the centre of the tree; weaker competitors should be cut away.

The deodar will grow in any reasonable soil. Propagation of the species is by seeds and of the varieties by grafting.

Celastrus scandens

CELASTRUS SCANDENS (Climbing bittersweet)

In its native countries this climbing bittersweet has the bad reputation of strangling trees completely and as a matter of fact in some languages the name is tree strangler. When planting it can be useful to remember this property.

With an amazing speed the plant will cover pergolas, garages or other buildings. The green foliage will smother everything and in autumn the bright orange seed mantles appear, breaking open after a short time and revealing the orange seeds in the interior, similar to the common spindle tree, which belongs to the same family. The attractive fruits make the branches very suitable for cutting and they will keep well indoors.

Though some experts maintain that the plant is bisexual, it is always useful to plant male and female plants together, in order to promote cross-fertilisation to get the most fruit. If the branches are wanted for cutting for house decoration this should be done before the fruits open.

On good soil and in a sunny place the shrub will produce root suckers that can be dug up and used for propagation. It is possible to use it on a north exposed wall.

Hard pruning will cause no damage. Propagation is also possible by layering the branches.

Chaenomeles speciosa 'Nivalis'   *C. japonica*   *Quince fruit*

CHAENOMELES (Japanese quince)

For a long time this plant was known as Cydonia and as a consequence it is still often labelled under that name. It is also widely known as Japonica.

Once well established the fine apple blossom flowers appear on the light green young shoots in March and often remain till the month of May. It can be grown as a shrub in a border or the branches can be trained flat against a wall. In autumn, after the leaves have fallen, the shrub often produces greenish-yellow fruits, very decorative in autumn flower arrangements or in a fruit bowl. They are edible and can be used for flavouring apple sauce when they are ripe; it is also possible to make them into jelly.

If the fruits fall off and ripen, birds are attracted to them. Around Christmas they may still be busy trying to reach the seeds inside.

The dense growth of the thorny branches make the quince an ideal hedge plant; it is completely hardy.

Pictured (above left) is the variety C. speciosa 'Nivalis', snow white as the name implies. The velvety dark red 'Simonii' is a slow grower and therefore welcome In smaller gardens. The bicoloured 'Crimson and Gold' has dark red flowers with conspicuous golden stamens; on account of its spreading branches it may be used as a ground covering plant.

Quinces thrive in any normal garden soil in the sun as well in half shade. They should not be planted too close to a path as they have thorny branches. As the flowers are produced on the previous year's growth, pruning should be limited to removing old and weak branches after flowering. Propagation is by cuttings or grafting.

41

Chamaecyparis obtusa 'Nana Gracilis'   *C. pisifera 'Squarrosa'*

CHAMAECYPARIS OBTUSA

One of the plants that is always admired by conifer lovers is the Japanese Hinoki cypress, Chamaecyparis obtusa 'Nana Gracilis', which is one of the many forms of this Japanese species.

This cypress is one of the most widely planted dwarf conifers. The broad pyramidical, semi-dwarf growth is exceptionally graceful and the shiny green foliage is extremely charming. As a consequence it can be the conversation piece of the rock garden. Sometimes small plants are used for edges of graves as they demand very little care.

Though a tough conifer, it has its limitations: it does not stand up to exposed positions or strong (sea) winds. Under poor circumstances it will lose its attractive shape. Moreover it is extremely sensitive to dogs' urine.

Little pruning is necessary. Sometimes thin, untypical, shoots should be trimmed away in summer. As this is a careful selected form of Chamaecyparis obtusa it can produce growths not true to type. Propagation by grafting and sometimes by cuttings is professional work.

In Japan, C. obtusa and its varieties are often used for making so called Bonsai trees, which are becoming very popular in Western Europe now. It is possible to keep a small specimen outdoors in an urn or window box, but cold winds can be fatal.

The other plant illustrated above is the woolly green C. pisifera 'Squarrosa', described on the next page.

Chamaecyparis pisifera 'Plumosa Aurea'   *C. p. 'Filifera Nana'*

CHAMAECYPARIS

Garden lovers often not know how to place the exotic Chamaecyparis varieties but nevertheless they can contribute a great deal to the decoration of the garden. It is a remarkable genus with leaves like overlapping scales on each side of the shoots, though there are varieties, mostly fixed juvenile forms, with needle-like leaves.

One of the many special forms of C. pisifera is C. p. 'Plumosa Aurea' (illustrated), a slow growing conical conifer with fern-like sprays that are yellow in spring, especially when they are young, and turn a bronze colour in winter. The broad growing pyramid is an effective centre-piece for a small lawn, at least it if is protected against the wind. Very bright golden yellow is C. p. 'Plumosa Flavescens' with a more prostrate growth; attractive too are C. pisifera 'Squarrosa' and the golden dwarf growing C. p. 'Plumosa Rogersii'.

C. p. 'Filifera Nana', shown above, is a remarkable plant with its dark green foliage hanging in long threads with few divisions, hence the name: filifera means 'thread forming'. It is good subject for a rock garden or in front of a conifer group. A fine yellow form is C. p. 'Filifera Aurea'.

These Chamaecyparis varieties have a pleasing natural form, so real pruning can be restricted to trimming away an odd branch in early summer. They will grow in most good garden soils, in particular with a little sand, and can be propagated by cuttings or grafting.

Chamaecyparis lawsoniana 'Stewartii'   *C. I. 'Triomph van Boskoop'*

CHAMAECYPARIS (Lawson cypress)

To botanists exploring California it was a great moment when they found a conical conifer of 150–180 feet, growing wild. In the same year, 1854, they sent seeds to Lawson's nursery in Edinburgh, and thus laid the foundation for a fine variable collection of garden conifers. Since then, out of the original C. lawsoniana seedlings many fine varieties have been selected: the blue-green 'Fletcher', and 'Ellwoodii', the slender upright 'Erecta', blue ones such as 'Allumii', and 'Triomphe de Boskoop', weeping trees such as 'Filiformis' and 'Pendula', and capricious 'Lycopoides', 'Minima' and 'Minima Glauca' are dwarfs and C. I. 'Stewartii', illustrated above, is a fine yellow conifer. Collectors know the merits of each. Some are ideal for the rock garden, others can yield branches for flower arrangements. The illustrated 'Stewartii' has a fine natural cone form and can be grown without any pruning; its leaves are golden yellow in summer and brownish in winter, but the interior is always greenish yellow. It is very hardy and will do as well in a small garden if branches are trimmed regularly; they are excellent for flower arranging.

If used as a hedge the plants should be given plenty of space or they cannot develop their characteristic shape.

Propagation is possible by seed and cuttings, but the finer varieties are always grafted.

44

Chamaecyparis obtusa 'Crippsii'

C. nootkatensis 'Glauca'

CHAMAECYPARIS

Those who enjoy making flower arrangements and seek a garden plant producing shoots for autumn compositions will find that C. obtusa 'Crippsii' makes an excellent choice. This variety is one of the many C. obtusa varieties, used for making Bonsai trees. The yellow foliage has the advantage of bringing colour into the winter garden; after a severe winter it may be necessary to cut off some brown tips.

Of quite another appearance is C. nootkatensis 'Glauca', illustrated on the right, originating from a forest tree native in Western America and named after an island near the Canadian West coast. The growth of this conifer is too vigorous for a small garden, but its extreme hardiness is a distinct advantage. As a matter of fact the name was winter cypress in olden times: Thuja borealis. Botanists of those days saw its hardiness as its most important quality.

Less fast growing is the fine weeping variety C. n. 'Pendula', with branches curving upwards and vertically hanging shoots at their ends. Such a conifer will look fine in the centre of a lawn, just as its yellow variety C. n. 'Aurea'.

All sandy soils are suitable. Propagation by grafting should be left to professionals.

Clematis 'Jackmanii'   *C. 'Nelly Moser'*   *C. 'Ville de Lyon'*

CLEMATIS (Large flowered)

Large flowering Clematis hybrids are real masterpieces of the art of breeding. The colours vary between pure white and dark violet, the flowers can be single or double, and it would be hard to make a choice of the finest variety.

Very attractive are 'Comtesse de Bouchaud', soft cyclamen pink, (June-September); 'Ernest Markham', velvety red (July-September); 'Gipsy Queen', velvety purple (July-September); 'Hybrida Sieboldi', lavender blue (July-August); 'Jackmanii', violet-blue (June-September); 'Lady Betty Balfour' rich voilet-blue (September-October); 'Lasurstern', purple-blue (May-June and September); 'Nelly Moser,' pink with mauve stripes (May-June and September); and 'Ville de Lyon', bright carmine red (July-September).

Clematis hybrids are always delivered in pots and can be planted at any time, except when there is snow on the ground, but it is important that the base of the stems at least is not exposed to the hot sun. If planted facing South it should be screened by a tile or a low plant. The roots should not have to compete with other plants, but even then it may take some time before Clematis is well established in its new position.

Though new shoots are made easily, pruning should be done with care; always cut back stem above a pair of buds. All newly planted Clematis should be cut back to within 6 inches of the ground after planting in early spring. This encourages strong new basal shoots. Future pruning depends on the type, but details are usually given in good plant catalogues. Propagation by cuttings is difficult, but stems can be layered in pots of sandy soil.

Clematis montana 'Tetrarose'

CLEMATIS (Small flowered)

Clematis are some of the most colourful plants of the garden, and once established attract much attention during their flowering time. They climb easily over fences and walls and, if unchecked, over other trees and plants with a nearly tropical tenacity.

Some small flowering species show well developed flower buds in April and the best known among them is C. montana, an extremely hardy native from the Himalaya, climbing up to 40 feet and flowering in May-June with white or pink flowers in large clusters.

Though the original species is very attractive, there are now several improved varieties, including the pink 'Elizabeth' and 'Tetrarose' with its extra large flowers.

Less well known, but very interesting, is C. tangutica, a fine yellow species with lantern-shaped flowers, flowering from June till September and showing fluffy seed heads afterwards that can be used in dried floral arrangements.

Our native clematis is C. vitalba or 'Travellers' Joy'. It can be seen rambling in hedges in the countryside. Seedlings of it are used for grafting large-flowered varieties.

Clematis succeed best in good, well manured soil, and one that does not dry out badly in the summer. Ideally the base of the plant should be screened with a low shrub, such as lavender.

Small flowering Clematis can be propagated by cuttings, or by layering.

Colutea arborescens   *Colutea (flowers and fruits)*

COLUTEA (Bladder senna)

This plant is a favourite with the children. For years they will remember the fun of making the 3 inches-long pods explode with a bang when they were squeezed.

It is by these pods, green at first and brownish later, that this tree-like shrub from Mediterranean areas is best known. It can grow to about 12 feet and it is made specially attractive by its long flowering period — from the end of May till September — giving a constant supply of pods for the children during that time. The yellow butterfly flowers contrast well with the bright green pinnate leaves; new ones appear every day and if the pods are not spoilt altogether by the children of the neighbourhood they turn brown and stay on the bush even after the flowers and leaves have gone.

Coluteas are not difficult to grow and are satisfied with any soil type. They can even be planted in poor soils where they will spread themselves by their seeds.

Pruning might be necessary if the base of the shrub becomes bare. Hard pruning might be done if the plants become too obtrusive. Propagation is by seeds sown directly after ripening, in a cold frame in autumn or in the garden in May. The seeds germinate very quickly and keep their germination power for years. It is also possible to multiply coluteas by softwood cuttings.

Cornus florida 'Rubra'

CORNUS (Dogwood or Cornel)

The number of species belonging to the genus Cornus is very large and rich in different forms. They are native to Asia and America and, on account of their varying leaves, bark colours and flowering systems, very interesting to botanists, but moreover to garden lovers.

Well known is C. mas, – yellow dogwood – native to Europe and flowering in February-March, about the same time as the witch hazel. Its branches can be brought inside and forced into flower in a vase.

This dogwood deserves more attention as it is an interesting winter flowering shrub.

The illustrated variety, C. florida 'Rubra', can be grown as a large shrub, or sometimes as a small tree. In autumn the leaves turn purple and orange. The flowers are inconspicuously green; its decorative value comes from the large white bracts, which are so much like flowers that many people think they are faced with a late flowering magnolia. The common C. florida has masses of white flowers in May.

From Japan comes C. kousa, flowering from May-June with white bracts that stay on the plant for several weeks; in a sunny, yet sheltered position, they are followed by strawberry-like fruits. The leaves have fine autumn colours.

Dogwoods need plenty of space and good soil. Propagation is by grafting or layering.

C. stolonifera 'Flaviramea' and C. alba 'Sibirica'   *Cornus alba 'Argenteomarginata'*

CORNUS (Dogwood)

In winter some of the dogwoods have brightly coloured, leafless stems. C. alba has blood-red young and greenish-red older branches which makes an unusual sight, particularly when snow is on the ground.

In summer this shrub is attractive as well, though the flowers are unimportant. Colour is provided by the leaves: the variety 'Argenteomarginata' has cream coloured edges, 'Gouchaultii' and 'Spaethii' have yellow ones. C. alba 'Kesselringii' has dark purple stems and looks very well together with C. stolonifera 'Flaviramea' with its bright green branches.

Several varieties of C. alba come from Siberia and Manchuria and are thus very hardy. Their attractions lie especially in winter. In a small garden they must be contained a little as they tend to throw out suckers. To enable the shrubs to produce the best coloured stems, all the growths should be cut back hard each March. Dogwood is an ideal plant to practise the old art of layering: young shoots can be bent to the ground and will root there if they are held by a peg or a bent wire. After a year the roots are sufficiently developed to enable the stem to live on its own, so it can be cut from the mother plant.

Corylopsis pauciflora

CORYLOPSIS PAUCIFLORA

The art of making an attractive garden is to ensure a long flowering period with a selection of plants interesting from early spring till late autumn. The smaller the garden, the more important the right choice.

Corylopsis pauciflora might contribute much in this respect. It came to us from China and Japan at the beginning of this century and has some similarity to the hazel (Corylus avellana) but has finer branches and a growth not much higher than 3 feet, an advantage in small gardens. The flowering is early, just like that of the witch hazel (Hamamelis mollis).

After winter, with rising temperatures, the 1—2 inches long bright yellow drooping racemas, reminding one of hops, will appear and though the scientific name means 'poor flowering' they will often remain for weeks, even during late frost or snow. Afterwards the leaves, reddish at first and bright green later on, will appear. In particular, after a warm and dry summer they will turn to beautiful autumn colours.

Corylopsis will do very well in combination with early flowering Rhododendron praecox and bulb flowers. Any humus containing soil is acceptable ; in a not too sunny position, and especially close to a warm wall, the plant should do well. Propagation is by cuttings.

Corylus avellana 'Contorta'

Corylus maxima 'Purpurea'

CORYLUS AVELLANA (Hazel)

Some plants are most attractive during their flowering period, others charm by their autumn colours or interesting fruits, but the corkscrew hazel (C. a. 'Contorta'), illustrated on the left, has its most glorious time when the inconspicuous leaves have disappeared and the capricious corkscrew growth is clearly seen. In particular older specimens prove to be a nearly inpenetrable tangle of curling shoots on which catkins appear in early spring. And it is interesting to note that this hazel is not a carefully planned result of hybridisation but is descended from a chance discovery in an English nursery.

The shrub can reach a height of 15 feet and should stand alone. The curled leaves are not – as many amateur gardeners are apt to suppose – a disease, but are natural to the variety. Propagation is possible by grafting on a normal hazel.

Another conspicuous variety is C. maxima 'Purpurea' that will grow strongly on any soil and produce catkins in spring and well formed reddish-brown leaves in summer. In a small garden it should be kept within bounds by hard pruning.

The plant is decorative on the edge of a lawn where the dark foliage nicely contrasts with the bright green grass. The purpose of pruning is to keep the hazel from overgrowing other plants. Even after hard pruning it will regain its old shape within a season.

Cotinus coggygria   *Cotinus coggygria 'Royal Purple'*

COTINUS COGGYGRIA (Smoke tree)

The common name 'smoke tree' applies to the typical loose feathered panicles of a length of 6–8 inches, bearing small purple flowers in July, part of the inflorescence being covered with silky hairs and together giving the impression of smoke clouds.

This is not the only attractive quality of the tree, which is a native of Mediterranean areas. The leaves turn to beautiful colours in the autumn and the young shoots are blood-red and keep this red tinge all through summer and winter. As a consequence this tree-like shrub is always attractive, in particular in sunlight and especially in winter. The flowers appear in June-July, while the smoke clouds stay a long time.

The other illustrated variety ,'Royal Purple', has very dark coloured leaves.

The smoke tree is vigorous and anything but particular about soil or place. Too rich a soil may unfavourably effect the autumn colours.

On account of its height, of about 10 feet, the smoke tree is best for the larger garden, unless stems are pruned hard each spring. This encourages young stems to be produced which have the best coloured foliage. Treated in this way the flowers are absent. Propagation is possible by layering lower branches.

C. salicifolia 'Floccosa'

Cotoneaster watereri 'Cornubia'

COTONEASTER

The genus Cotoneaster consists of about 50 species of hardy evergreen and deciduous shrubs, ranging from prostrate mat forming types to large bushes and even trees.

Among the taller evergreen types C. salicifolia 'Floccosa', illustrated above, is a variety that stays attractive throughout the year. The long, somewhat arching, branches retain their glossy green willow-like leaves nearly all winter, but they turn brown later in the season. In June 3 inches wide corymbs of white flowers appear, much later followed by clusters of red berries, lasting till January and often bending the branches under their weight thus giving a quite different appearance to the shrub. The berried branches last well in water indoors.

There are several varieties of this cotoneaster, suitable for the large as well as for the small garden. 'Parkteppich' and 'Repens' are notable as they have prostrate branches and can serve as ground cover plants; their berries are less numerous than on the erect growing varieties. C. 'Cornubia' has strong less arching, branches and grows to a height of up to 20 feet; its leaves are large and its many berries stay on the plant till January.

Cotoneasters grow everywhere, even in dark shade, but if a good crop of berries are wanted a sunny place will be better.

Propagation is possible by seed, but to have plants true to type cuttings are better.

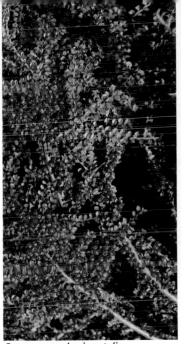

Cotoneaster horizontalis

C. dammeri

COTONEASTER HORIZONTALIS

This dense, wide shrub, branching herring-bone fashion, easily reaches a height of 20 inches without support. In autumn the glossy dark green leaves turn purplish red and the berries can be so numerous that they nearly hide the whole shrub. It is an ideal plant to be grown against walls under the window sill, as they climb without support. A plant will reach up to 7 feet even against north eastern walls.

C. h. 'Robusta' is sturdier and will reach 5 feet without any support. The large leaves turn to fine colour shades in autumn.

A good plant for carpeting banks and bare ground is C. dammeri, reaching 6 inches at the most and spreading even over walls. In severe winters part of the foliage is lost but grows again in spring.

A new variety of C. dammeri is 'Skogholm', originating from Sweden, with a prostrate growth but somewhat higher than the species described above. The Scandinavian origin points to hardiness; the plant is even ideal for ground cover. The variety 'Coral Beauty' has the same qualities and more berries.

Cotoneasters are satisfied with any soil and place. Propagation is possible from seeds and cuttings, but only by the latter method will the new plant resemble its parent. Layering is another useful method of propagation.

Crataegus oxyacantha 'Pauls' Scarlet'

CRATAEGUS (Hawthorn)

All garden centre proprietors know that their customers have a sentimental attraction to the hawthorn. They always have it in stock as gardeners keep asking for them, probably due to happy memories of an old farmhouse where hawthorn in flower left a deep impression.

Hawthorns are grown as shrubs, as trees and, in particular, as hedges, especially in western France, England and Ireland. The hedges are shaped by pruning and are made inpenetrable in that way.

Very attractive is C. oxyacantha, especially in May-June when numerous clusters of sweet-scented flowers nearly smother the young green shoots. The red variety, 'Paul's Scarlet', is effective as a shrub as well as a tree.

The common hawthorn, C. monogyna, is pleasing, especially around a house in rural surroundings. It flowers two weeks later than the above named variety and is resistant to salt and air pollution; the clusters of white sweet-scented flowers stay undamaged. Three to six young plants per yard make a nice thick hedge within two years.

Hawthorn grows almost everywhere, even close to the sea, though prevailing winds can deform the plant to one side. It can take a lot of pruning, but it is useful to remember that it flowers on the branches of the previous year.

Propagation is by cuttings or grafting as seeds germinate very slowly, if at all.

Cryptomeria japonica   *C. j. 'Bandai-Sugi'*

CRYPTOMERIA JAPONICA (Japanese cedar)

A botanical curiosity is the Cryptomeria genus as only one species is known. In Japan this conifer is an important source of timber and a conspicuous feature of the landscape. The bark of the hardy tree is orange-brown and the leaves are wide spreading. The fast growing stem is very flexible and moves elegantly in the wind, which makes the tree specially attractive when standing alone.

Cryptomeria japonica, brought to the West together with many other plants in the nineteenth century, is exceptionably variable and as a consequence nurserymen have selected many interesting forms. From the original C. japonica derive 'Compacta', a strong grower with dark green foliage, and 'Bandai-Sugi', an irregular growing dwarf, green in summer, bronze in winter. Something of special interest to lovers of unusual plants is 'Cristata', an erect grower with remarkable fastigiate branches, often with the appearance of a cock's comb and extremely suitable for modern flower arrangements.

Very hardy is 'Globosa Nana', a broad round topped bush with dense mid-green foliage, that keeps its colour very well in winter. This variety is suitable for the rock garden, as also is 'Vilmoriniana', a slowly growing globe that turns brown in winter which makes people think that the plant has some disease, but the colour is restored in spring.

Cryptomerias are resistant to wind, need no pruning, and are propagated by grafting and cuttings.

Cupressocyparis leylandii

CUPRESSOCYPARIS LEYLANDII

All over the world nurserymen keep hybridising in the hope of finding a new plant with large commercial possibilities. Yet many remarkable plants do not owe their existence to industrious nurserymen, but are products of pure chance, accidental crosses or mutations.

In particular, in the conifer world, accidental hybridisation gave birth to some surprising results. Among them is Cupressocyparis Leylandii, illustrated above, a cross between Cupressus macrocarpa, a not very hardy conifer, and Chamaecyparis nootkatensis, a very hardy conifer described on page 45.

Most specimens we have now are descendants of seedlings found in 1888 and 1911. Some of the best cultivars now grown are 'Green Spire', 'Leighton Green' and 'Haggetson Grey'.

C. leylandii is extremely hardy and a fast grower on most soils. This makes it an excellent hedging plant, especially if a good height within a short time is required. It can also be used as a solitary tree; it will grow faster and is more decorative than the well-known Chamaecyparis lawsoniana. It is one of the fastest growing conifers in the British Isles and tolerates exposure, particularly near the sea.

This greyish-green, densely growing, conifer is very decorative. It will do well in any soil. Propagation is simple; only short cuttings are needed to be rooted in sandy soil in a propagating frame.

Cytisus praecox *C. p. 'Hollandia'*

CYTISUS PRAECOX (Broom)

This broom is another wonder of nature. Experts believe that C. praecox is a cross between long forgotten species from the Mediterranean region, for instance C. multiflorus and C. purgans, made by an unknown nurseryman a long time ago. From these inconspicuous sub-tropical ancestors we have now a hardy plant, flowering in April to May, starting cream coloured and turning yellow, reaching a height of about 6 feet.

This flowering period being the same as that of Japanese azaleas, growing it in combination with the latter's red and purple varieties is effective, and with some bright green conifers in the background a fine colour symphony of spring flowers can be achieved. Also, planted with late tulip varieties, this broom makes an attractive combination. It needs very little attention.

The scent of the flowers is extremely strong and may give people a headache when brought indoors.

The variety 'Albus' has a lower growth and arching shoots. Brooms like full sun and do best in comparitively poor loamy garden soil. As the plants flower on the previous seasons shoots only older branches should not be pruned. Only cut back the younger growths just as the flowers fade. Propagation is possible by cuttings or grafting.

Cytisus scoparius 'Firefly'

CYTISUS SCOPARIUS (Common broom)

The common broom is native to Western Europe, but has been cultivated as a garden plant for centuries. In severe winters, and in exposed places with strong sunlight after frost, it might die back to the ground, but will revive in the next season. The plant, with its fine yellow flowers standing singly or in pairs, fits nicely in the landscape and is especially suitable for natural and heather gardens.

However, gardeners were not satisfied with the attractions of the original species and after breeding and selecting they found a number of new varieties in all kinds of shades. For example, 'Golden Sunlight' is the shade of white wine, 'Andreanus' is bicoloured: the flag of the flower is deep yellow and the wings have a brown blotch. 'Dragonfly' has a deep yellow flag with brown wings and a pure yellow keel; this variety grows very slowly and is therefore suitable for small gardens. One of the finest varieties is 'Fulgens', with orange-yellow flag and brown wings. If space is available a group of different varieties is very effective.

Brooms grow best in light soil with leaf mould; combined with upright junipers and birches they make a very attractive feature.

The species can be propagated by seeds; the varieties by cuttings or grafting.

Daphne mezereum

DAPHNE MEZEREUM (Mezereon)

The moment that the pink flower buds of the mezereon unfold depends on the severity of the proceeding winter. If it has been mild it might be in February, but they can wait till April after a long, cold period.

During the flowering season they give out a strong scent and as a consequence bumble bees and even butterflies visit them, coming over great distance and in large numbers. In very old books the mezereon is recommended as a bee plant.

In the past this slow growing, erect, little bush suffered very much from a chronic and very persistant virus infection, but since then growers have overcome this problem. From the very variable species a number of selections were made, such as 'Ruby Glow', with large purple-red flowers in greater numbers than with the original species. 'Select', too, has large purple flowers. The improvement in health and appearance no doubt will make the mezereon a more popular garden plant.

As the mezereon likes lime and chalk in the soil it will grow best in soil unsuitable for heather, rhododendrons and azaleas. Though a woodland plant by nature it appreciates a sunny place. Pruning is hardly necessary and should be limited to removing old mossy branches. Propagation is possible from seeds which should be sown in autumn, as soon as possible after riping. Families with children should know that the attractive red berries are poisonous.

Deutzia gracilis

Deutzia gracilis 'Mont Rose'

DEUTZIA

The different varieties of Deutzia are an interesting group of ornamental shrubs with the climax of the flowering period in June. The illustrated variety, D. gracilis, might even start flowering about mid-May. The white flowers combine very well with more vivid colours, e.g. of roses, late rhododendrons, kolkwitzias and weigelas, to mention some of the plants described elsewhere in this book. A good landscape architect will make use of this.

Deutzia gracilis is a bushy shrub reaching a height of 3–4 feet, and the pure white flowers are borne in erect racemes. The variety 'Mont Rose' has a more upright growth than other members of the family and larger panicles of purplish-pink flowers with bright yellow stamens, flowering in June.

Interesting too, are the lower 'Kalmiaeflora' and the higher 'Magnifica' with large dense plumes.

All of them like sunny positions and heavy rich soil. Pruning immediately after flowering is important, but as the flowers appear on the previous year's growth only older branches should be removed to promote full flowering the next year.

Propagation is possible by hardwood and softwood cuttings.

Eleagnus angustifolia   *E. ebbingei*

ELEAGNUS (Oleaster)

Owners of gardens near to the sea and exposed to persistant cold and often salty winds may have problems in finding suitable plants for their garden in which the soil can be poor. Improvement then is only possible by bringing in good garden soil – an expensive solution.

Here Eleagnus angustifolla – Oleaster – can be of great help, originating as it does from poor soil in Mediterranean countries or Asiatic steppes where it grows very well.

Its stiff leaves, covered with silvery hairs at the back, indicate their resistance to sea winds.

Oleasters can be used as a wind breaking hedge even in places where other plants might perish. Weaker plants find protection behind it and thus survive. Also in its favour is the fact that the oleaster does not make any suckers or runners and takes hard pruning very well. Moreover silvery flowers appear in June, attracting many bees by their scent. In autumn the edible silver-amber fruit appears even in situations where other plants find it hard to live.

This remarkable plant, which makes no demands, can reach a height of 20 feet if not pruned and may be propagated from seeds.

A good evergreen and a better form is E. ebbingei with silvery-grey leathery leaves. This plant is also suitable for places close to the sea, but in northern regions it might be cut back in severe weather.

Enkianthus campanulatus

ENKIANTHUS CAMPANULATUS

People living in areas with peaty soil are often inspired by their environment to make a heather garden. The plants need not be restricted to calluna and erica varieties ; there are a great many others that will be at home in the same conditions. Among them is Enkianthus campanulatus. It is a broad growing shrub from Japan that can reach a height of 7 feet.

The branches are whorled, the shiny leaves growing in clusters at the end of the shoots look evergreen, but nevertheless they are shed after turning brilliant red, in particular after a dry summer. In May the plant bears creamy yellow flowers with red veins, reminding one of lily-of-the-valley flowers, in pendulous terminal racemes.

Being a leggy plant with very few branches, Enkianthus is not attractive in a solitary position, especially in winter, but it is very much at home in a heather garden. Like all Ericaceae it needs lime-free soil and will appreciate peat or peat moss in its planting hole and in winter will like some protection at the foot of the plant.

The plant never needs any pruning.

Propagation is possible from cuttings of side shoots, placed in a cold frame in autumn.

Group Erica with Juniperus

ERICA (Heather)

There are a great many kinds which are invaluable low-growing shrubs, and if planted fairly close together soon form a dense carpet and smother weeds. As a result they have become very popular as ground-cover plants. Despite this, weeds do grow between them, and until they are well established careful attention must be given to weeding. Most heathers need lime-free soil, although some of the winter-flowering kinds, such as Erica carnea, will tolerate a little lime. Preparation of the soil for all types, including Calluma (ling), should include adding liberal quantities of moist peat to the soil.

Good varieties, flowering between November and May, are E. carnea 'Aurea' (lilac pink flowers and golden foliage), 'Ruby Glow' (deep purple pink), 'Snow Queen' (pure white) and 'Winter Beauty' (dark purple pink).

From June until October flowers may be expected on E. cinerea 'Alba' (white flowers), 'C. D. Eason' (fiery red), 'Pallas' (fine purple), E. vagans 'St. Keverne' (salmon pink).

Besides heather one needs other plants to create a natural heather landscape, such as Juniperus communis, Kalmia, Andromeda and Enkianthus described elsewhere. Birches may give a vertical dimension to the garden.

Winter flowering varieties of erica should be trimmed back with shears in April, the others in late summer. Propagation is by cuttings of young shoots in summer and layering.

Euonymus europaea *E. alata (in autumn)*

EUONYMUS (Spindle tree)

The spindle tree is native to Europe and it can be used in a border or in woodland conditions.

E. europaeus is very decorative on account of its remarkable fruits. Even at a tender age the shrub's pinkish fruits attract attention, in particular when they are ripe and the orange seeds come dangling out. Moreover fine autumn shades contribute to the beauty of the garden for weeks; cut branches may be used indoors.

E. europaeus is completely hardy and is at home in a soil with humus and lime; plants stand drought very well. Improved varieties are 'Aldenhamensis', with long stemmed bright pink fruits, 'Atrorubens' with dark carmine-red fruits, and 'Red Cascade' with a profusion of bright red fruits on arching branches.

The other illustrated species, E. alata, has corky 'wings' on its stiff branches as its most conspicuous feature; even on young plants they may be found opposite to each other and changing direction at every bud, giving the impression that the branches are four winged. The flowers are unimportant and the plant, being unisexual and with nearly all specimens male, fruits are rare. Still the plant comes to full beauty in autumn, the leaves turning pale pink to dark red; it is only a pity that this period is so short.

E. alata prefers a sunny position; in the shade the corky wings stay rudimentary. It has fine autumn colours. Pruning is not necessary and propagation is by cuttings.

Euonymus fortunei 'Gracilis'

EUONYMUS FORTUNEI

The illustrated plant is well known as it is often used for edging and also sold as an indoor plant. Until a few years ago the usual name was E. radicans 'Argenteomarginata' and it may still be offered under this name.

In a position close to a wall the plant is apt to climb; in particular in sunny and fertile places it may even reach a great height, though it is not a natural climber.

E. fortunei is very decorative ,sometimes producing pure white leaves. Green shoots should be cut away in order to prevent the plant from turning green completely. Though a sunny position is most favoured the plant stands half-shade very well and thus may be planted under higher trees.

A large leaved variety is E. f. 'Silver Gem', a shrub with white edged leaves ,and also capable of climbing. During winter and in cold exposed positions it might be damaged.

A stronger variety is E. fortunei 'Vegeta' with green leaves, which is capable of spreading through the garden by means of rooting shoots. At a later age characteristic fruits with dangling orange seeds will appear, even in the shade. Still more fruits may be expected from E. f. 'Carrierei', a strong grower without rooting runners.

All described varieties grow in normal garden soil. Prune only when they get too high; propagation is easy from cuttings.

Forsythia intermedia 'Lynwood Gold'

FORSYTHIA

This is a highly popular early spring flowering shrub. It seems to be stimulated by winter cold, and as a consequence it shows its golden profusion in March or April, when other plants are still bare. In summer they disappear in soft green anonymity, after having played, as it were, the overture to the summer symphony. Stems cut in bud will soon open their blossoms indoors.

The shrub was named after William Forsyth (1737–1804), who was the royal gardener at Kensington Palace. The best known variety is F. intermedia 'Spectabilis', a strong growing upright shrub with large golden yellow flowers. The newer 'Lynwood Gold' is still brighter yellow, and 'Beatrix Farrand', with flowers over 2 inches, is certainly a valuable newcomer.

Forsythias often need some seasons to get established, but finally they will grow in any good garden soil, but they need some sunshine; in too shady a place the branches will be thin.

Pruning should be done sparingly. Stems that have flowered can be cut back as the flowers fade; dead branches should be cut away. Propagation is easy by hard wood cuttings taken in early autumn and rooted outside.

Gaultheria procumbens

GAULTHERIA PROCUMBENS (Partridge Berry, Wintergreen)

Many owners of small gardens are constantly looking for low plants and as a conse-quence the demand for them is often greater than for taller shrubs. Moreover the search is for ground covering plants, in particular for those that grow in the shade. Here Gaultheria procumbens can give very satisfactory results as this creeping plant will not grow higher than 6 inches. Its dark green leathery leaves have a length of about an inch and are clustered at the end of the shoots. The leaves, often somewhat reddish, have fine autumn colours but still are not ched in winter. In July-August small white flowers appear, and while these are still present the first small red fruits follow. As birds do not like the fruit these often stay on the plants well into spring.

Around Christmas plenty may be sold in pots for indoor decoration.

On account of the soil requirements — much humus and no lime — Gaultheria fits well in the heather garden. In half shade the plants are liable to form a matted growth by means of rooted runners.

A more vigorous shrub is G. shallon, coming from Western America. It may reach 3 feet. It has greener leaves but less conspicuous dark purple berries. People with a garden on peaty soil will find it a fast ground-covering plant.

Pruning is seldom necessary. Propagation is simple : rooted runners may be cut off and planted elsewhere. Division, too, is possible.

69

Genista tinctoria

GENISTA (Broom)

Genista has much in common with Cytisus. The main difference is that the trifoliate leaves of Genista stay long, while those of Cytisus drop off early.

There is a good choice of variety and it is possible to have genistas in flower from April until far into summer. The first to open are the small flowers of creeping G. pilosa, the yellow terminal racemes of which keep appearing until August. The prostrate shrub will not grow higher than 6-8 inches. Being satisfied with any soil and forming close mats of whip-like shoots, it is very suitable for the heather garden.

In June G. tinctoria – Dyer's greenwood – opens its yellow flowers. This native shrub can reach a height of 25 inches. A lower variety, 'Royal Gold', has a semi-globular form, prostrate growth and long trusses of yellow flowers from June until August.

A real plant of the dry Mediterranean region is C. hispanica, the Spanish gorse, densely spined and hairy with flowers in May-June, a real guest for the rockery. More prosperous looking is 'Lydia', originating from Syria with arching rich flowering branches, making the plant suitable to hang from walls and embankments. In a sunny position it will be satisfied with any poor soil, but it will grow as well in good soil. Pruning should be limited to cutting the tops after flowering, thus promoting a bushy growth.

Propagation of all varieties is by cuttings.

Ginkgo biloba

GINKGO BILOBA (Maidenhair Tree)

Family, genus and species are united in this one tree. At first sight it looks like a deciduous tree, but Ginkgo biloba belongs to the Gymnospermes, more or less related to the conifers.

In Japan this remarkable tree has been honoured in many ways and legends and as a consequence in the past women prayed under it for the blessing of a large family. The hairy stem which always feels warm like the human body, and the mammary growths, that appear when the tree gets older, have undoubtedly contributed to this mystic association.

This tree will be of great interest in a somewhat large garden though it might look a little skinny at first. The fan-shaped leaves, waved at the edges, turn to a beautiful golden colour before they drop off in autumn.

If planted young at a height of about 3 feet, it will not need any support and though it will grow well in a normal garden soil it will appreciate some good leafmould or compost around the base.

A maidenhair tree should not be pruned at all as the branches will not sprout again and might even die back. The oldest specimen in Europe is in the university garden of Leiden, Holland ; it is some three hundred years old, yet still retains a fine natural shape.

Ginkgos exist also in weeping form, but they are rare. The tree is unisexual ; the females produce slippery nuts and therefore only the males are used as avenue trees ; moreover their shape is better.

Propagation is possible from seeds imported from Japan.

Gleditsia triacantha

GLEDITSIA TRIACANTHOS (Honey locust)

It must have been quite a shock to travelling botanists when they discovered a full grown specimen of the honey locust in America. Indeed it is a remarkable tree, trunk and branches being armed with long, simple and even branched spines. It can reach a height of 30 feet and the spines can be as long as 15 inches.

Of course an adult specimen is only suitable for a park, but nevertheless it deserves the attention of plant lovers. An advantage is that small song birds are safe in the crown where cats and other animals cannot possibly reach their nests.

It is possible to use the honey locust as a hedging plant by keeping the stems pruned hard, but it will be a very spiny one. The brittle branches make the tree unsuitable for windy regions.

In June-July clusters of green butterfly flowers appear that strongly attract bees. In autumn the flowers are followed by long pods of up to 12 inches, hanging gracefully on the branches.

A more modest shrub form is G. triacanthos 'Elegantissima', a compact, slow-growing variety with fern-like leaves and without spines. From the United States came the new 'Sunburst' with golden yellow foliage turning greenish in summer.

The honey locust is at home in any soil and can be propagated by seeds; the varieties need grafting.

Hamamelis mollis   *H. japonica 'Arborea'*

HAMAMELIS (Witch hazel)

In winter sun the ribbon-like petals of the witch hazel can unfold before Christmas, but generally the brown felt-like buds open in a non-freezing period of January or February. Should it freeze or snow again the ribbons coil up and wait for better times, be it for weeks and covered with snow; in this position they even can stand 20 °C of frost.

In a protected position, cold winds do not get a chance to dry out the flowers and there a witch hazel comes to full and long lasting glory. The slow growth makes it also a good plant for small gardens; there, too, it gives much pleasure for years. An attractive colour combination may be obtained by planting winter flowering heathers at the base of the plant.

The best known species is H. mollis; the soft scent of its bright yellow flowers even lures insects out of their holes in the middle of the winter. Of somewhat looser habit and with less conspicuous flowers is the H. japonica 'Arborea'; it is wider spreading, with thinner shoots, and the flowers are pale sulphur yellow suffused with red, opening somewhat earlier.

New varieties are 'Feuerzauber', with bronze tinted flowers, and 'Jelena', a strong grower with yellow to orange flowers – undoubtedly plants with good prospects.

A witch hazel will grow anywhere. Flowering on the wood of the previous year it should hardly be pruned. Only if the shape calls for some correction it may be pruned sparingly just before flowering; the cut branches are fit for indoor use and even keep their scent there.

Propagation is by grafting on seedling rootstocks.

Hedera helix　　　　　　　　　　　　　　　　*H. h. 'Arborescens'*

HEDERA (Ivy)

When the autumn winds have blown away the leaves of deciduous trees and shrubs, one notices that there are few evergreen climbers and then ivy is appreciated more than ever.

In summer this climber is not very conspicuous, but in winter its qualities are more obvious, for not only does it cover old walls and fences so effectively, it also makes banks attractive. Where other plants perish through lack of light, the ivy goes on laying its mosaic of dark green leaves. With its little aerial rootlets the plant climbs the steepest obstacles. Ivy is not appreciated as much as it should be and some people feel it can harm buildings, but this has never been proved.

Ivy grows on all soils and can transform a tree trunk into a fine green column, but it should be pruned back before it reaches the top of the trunk.

A hardy variegated ivy is H. colchica 'Dentatavariegata'. A small leaved variety is H. helix 'Hibernica', the Irish ivy. Another variation is H.h. 'Arborescens', a shrubby form propagated by making cuttings of the arborescent growth of H. helix produced when the runner reaches the top of its support and starts flowering. Even the foliage is different, which may be seen in the photograph on the right.

Pruning ivy is only necessary if it becomes too unruly. Propagation is easy by cuttings and runners.

Hibiscus syriacus 'Coelestis'   *H. s. 'Woodbridge'*

HIBISCUS SYRIACUS (Rose of Sharon)

This plant has been under cultivation so long that there are no wild forms left. Centuries ago travellers found only cultivated varieties in Chinese and Japanese gardens.

As a garden plant Hibiscus is becoming more and more appreciated, probably because indoor types are so popular and perhaps also for the reason that tourists abroad see them in warm countries where they grow outdoors into plants of large size and are often used to line streets.

By the 16th century H. syriacus was a garden plant in England. In a cold wet summer the development of the flowers is slow, but under favourable conditions new flowers appear every day from the end of July until the beginning of October.

There are many attractive varieties such as the fine blue 'Coelestis', the red 'Rubis', and the rosy-red 'Woodbridge'. 'Admiral Dewey' is pure white, and of the same colour, but livelier because of its red blotches, is 'Speciosus'. These are only some of the finer varieties; experience has taught us that single varieties are best in colder areas.

As to the soil, hibiscus is not very particular but it likes a sunny position protected against cold dry winds; in colder areas it is barely hardy.

Restraint should be practised when pruning. The plant, which can reach a height of over six feet, should be given a chance of establish itself. Later shoots may be pruned a little to preserve the shape of the plant. Though flowering on the current year's shoots, Hibiscus does not stand hard pruning.

Propagation is by grafting on its own roots or on understock.

Hippophae rhamnoides

HIPPOPHAE RHAMNOIDES (Sea buckthorn)

The popular name for this plant clearly tells us that it is a thorny plant, at home by the seaside. It is native of Europe and the temperate parts of Asia, and is important for its faculty of binding soil against wind erosion in sandy areas close to the sea. It is, in fact, satisfied with any poor soil and thrives even in sand, apparently without nutrients. Even after being covered completely by sand storms it will revive.

The flowering of this shrub, which has separate male and female plants, is very inconspicuous. Not before late in autumn, when bright orange berries appear, can it be certain that a particular plant is female. Like other unisexual plants – pernettyas and many hollies – there should be a male specimen in the neighbourhood in order to ensure fruits on the female ones. One male plant can pollinate six or more females.

It is regrettable that the fruits, extremely rich in vitamin C, are enjoyed by the birds which strip the shrubs later in the season.

Even in exposed positions where all other plants have given up, the sea buckthorn will grow and even develop to a small tree, sometimes up to 30 feet. The runners, useful as they are in binding the soil, may be a nuisance in the normal garden. Therefore pruning should be done mainly under the ground and can be limited to the runners.

Propagation is by seeds.

Hydrangea arborescens 'Grandiflora'

HYDRANGEA ARBORESCENS 'GRANDIFLORA' (American hydrangea)

Many species of hydrangea are known. They are natives of Central and Eastern Asia, including the Himalayas, and North and South America. They were cultivated in Japan and China centuries before they were introduced into England by Sir Joseph Banks in 1789. This species originates from the Eastern United States.

In our gardens we now find the improved variety 'Grandiflora' in which the flowers are double. The number of flowers and the size of the heads can be so great that after rain the branches break under their weight. Every fast growing shoot bears a large corymb that can reach a diameter of six inches on good, well manured soil.

In July, at the start of the flowering season, the florets are creamy coloured; later they turn greenish-white. That colour persists until the end of the flowering period in September; afterwards it is better to cut off the flower heads.

Unlike others, this very hardy shrub should not be pruned till early spring and then not too severely. The flowers develop from lateral shoots arising on the long strong branches. If the plants should be cut back too far flowering may not occur. The shoots can be pruned to just above the highest strong bud. If the interior of the shrub becomes somewhat crowded, older thick branches can be cut away completely.

With a height of about 6 feet, this hydrangea is specially suitable for larger gardens and it will also grow under trees.

Propagation is by division or cuttings.

Hydrangea paniculata 'Grandiflora'

HYDRANGEA PANICULATA 'GRANDIFLORA'

This is a highly impressive shrub that may keep its flowers up to four months of the year, no doubt an advantage to people with little time for gardening.

The type called 'Grandiflora' was brought to Europe by Von Sieboldt, who found it in Japan about 1867. If it is given plenty of space the plant will flower very freely with massive panicles of sterile florets appearing in summer and autumn, first creamy white and nicely contrasting with the green grass and foliage, later turning to darker shades to nearly red in autumn. They even remain after the leaves have fallen; when cut they can be used for indoor decoration.

For people who like to use their pruning secateurs this is an ideal plant as pruning back to two inches from the growth of the previous year, and even deeper, induces the plant to give more flowers. Weak shoots should be taken away completely and strong ones cut down to three buds. Pruning should be done in early March.

The hydrangea enjoys a sunny position in lime free soil. It is very hardy and can stand exposed situations. Propagation is possible by cuttings and grafting on the roots.

Hydrangea petiolaris

HYDRANGEA PETIOLARIS (Climbing hydrangea)

This climbing hydrangea is a pleasing exception to the more usual range of hydrangea shrubs, with pink or blue flowers. Grown even on the north side of a wall, strong branches with thick bunches of aerial roots make it possible for the plant to climb remarkably quickly. Just like ivy it will cover tree trunks, walls and fences, be it at a slower speed. Only if a surface is smooth need wires be provided to give the branches some assistance.

It may also be grown in a rock garden, sending out running shoots over the ground and surrounding obstacles.

In June–July the creamy coloured, saucer-like corymbs appear bearing an edge of large sterile flowers around a centre of fertile florets, often hiding the plant completely. After the flowering period the ovate bright green leaves appear again, and in winter the picturesque light brown branches still provide an attractive sight.

Hydrangea petiolaris is the latest of the many scientific names this plant has had in the past, such as H. scandens and H. anomala petiolaris; it has much in common with Schizophragma hydrangeoides. The plant is very hardy and likes fertile, moist soil. Pruning is not necessary and propagation is by cuttings.

Hypericum calycinum

HYPERICUM (St. John's wort)

There are more than four hundred (generally herbaceous) representatives of this large genius to be found in the northern hemisphere. Some woody forms are suitable for the garden and deserve more attention than they have received up until now.

Because of its many good properties Hypericum calycinum can be a great asset, the leaves staying on the plant in winter, thus enlivening the bare season. Its height of 12 inches makes it suitable for a small garden, while its numerous runners make it a good choice for ground cover.

The plant flowers profusely from June until September, and the golden yellow flowers with conspicuous stamens can measure 3 inches across. As it also thrives in the shade, it can be grown successfully under trees and shrubs.

A plant with so many good qualities, and in addition is satisfied with all kinds of soil, can be considered ideal for every garden. It was a happy botanical event when explorers brought a specimen to Europe from Asia Minor in the seventeenth century.

Well-known varieties are H. patulum 'Henryi' which grows higher than H. calycinum but has smaller flowers, and H. 'Hidcote' which can reach a height of 5 feet and has larger leaves, partly shed in winter, and large golden-yellow flowers.

Soil or position will not present any problems and as a rule pruning is not necessary. H. calycinum can be kept in trim by hard pruning every few years in spring. Propagation is by runners and cuttings.

Ilex aquifolium 'J. C. van Tol'   *I. a. 'Aureomarginata'*

ILEX AQUIFOLIUM (Holly)

The numerous, generally red, berries in late autumn and its use as a Christmas decoration make holly attractive and well known. Gardeners wanting berried branches in their home and not wishing to purchase hideous plastic imitations should ensure that they have both male and female holly trees, this being necessary to ensure berries, as the plants are unisexual.

Holly is native to western Europe and is grown generally throughout the whole world. In ancient times the plant, together with other tooth-leaved species, was registered under the genus Aquifolium but this name is now used for the species of common holly.

Not all hollies have toothed leaves; the plant is extremely variable in leaf forms and colours. They may be found with saw-edged as well as smooth-edged leaves, silver and gold variegated ones and leaves with yellow edges. The greater part of these varieties have few or no berries.

A well-known, strong growing berried variety is 'J. C. van Tol' with dark, shiny, often hardly toothed leaves and large berries, of which the red may have an orange tinge. An advantage to gardeners is that the berries are eaten by birds only in long and cold winters. The common holly offers tastier fruits and should therefore be cut weeks before Christmas or covered with netting, or the birds will not leave a single berry.

The fertility is variable. Though holly is a forest plant, naturally growing in the shade under trees, it grows as well in the sun. Propagation is by seeds or cuttings. Under established plants seedlings ready for transplanting may often be found.

Ilex crenata 'Golden Gem'

ILEX CRENATA

Ilex crenata is completely different from the other prickly leaved species. Generally it is grown as a compact shrub growing to about 7 feet, either as a solitary specimen or in a hedge.

The tiny leaves are not larger than one inch and shallowly toothed; the inconspicuous flowers are followed by black fruits. In a small garden the new variety 'Golden Gem' will give much pleasure; its golden leaves keep ther icolour even in winter. I.c. 'Convexa', with a height of 3 feet and a spread of 2–3 feet, is extremely hardy and may be used in groups or as a hedge.

Among the other hollies, I. verticillata is a remarkable species. It is a deciduous species of which the branches are sold commercially for decoration purposes in autumn and especially around Christmas. It is, moreover, a fine garden plant but, just as with I. aquifolium, male and female plants are needed if berries are wanted and it is a pity that the males do not have a good habit of growth.

Birds love the berries and therefore netting will be necessary to protect them. The plant will not feel at home in a chalky soil.

In general hollies will grow in every garden soil and all do best in the sun. Varieties can be propagated by cuttings, species by seeds that need to be stratified as they often germinate very slowly.

Jasminum nudiflorum

JASMINUM NUDIFLORUM (Winter jasmine)

In a mild frost-free autumn the first soft yellow flowers of the winter jasmine may appear in November. As long as there is no frost new flowers open every day, but the beginning and end of the flowering season differ from year to year; still in mild winters it may last from November until April. The fact that it flowers during this season makes winter jasmine an attractive plant, even for the small garden. Only in severe winters and in exposed places is flowering hindered.

The best position for the shrub, which is often classified as a climber on account of its limp branches, is on a southern wall. With a support, and grown in association with ivy, it can easily reach 15 feet.

It is also possible to grow the plant hanging from a wall or as a ground cover, the branches rooting easily and spreading many feet from the original position, sometimes combining with branches of surrounding shrubs.

Winter jasmine is not fussy about soil or position. Pruning of well-trained plants consists of cutting back stems that have flowered fairly close to their base once the blossoms have fallen. It is possible to force branches into flower indoors.

Propagation is simple by cuttings and runners.

Juniperus communis 'Hibernica'   *J. sabina var. tamariscifolia*   *J. virg. 'Skyrocket'*

JUNIPERUS (Juniper)

There are so many species, forms and varieties of Juniperus that a collector might spend a life time in finding them. There are columnar forms and creeping species in many colours and, moreover, the leaves can be absolutely different. Altogether a real playground to botanists, but to the ordinary gardener they are important elements in his garden.

The illustrated J. communis 'Hibernica' – the Irish juniper – is a blue-grey form of the common juniper, found all over Europe and across Asia and North-America. The shrub can provide the additional dimension of height to the rockery or the heather garden where it will be very much at home.

Entirely different is J. sabina 'Tamariscifolia', illustrated as well. It is a creeping plant with dark to blue-green foliage and creeping branches. This variety is also suitable for the rockery and for growing wild in larger gardens. Pruning is seldom needed.

To those wanting to add a Mediterranean atmosphere to their garden, and looking for some hardy substitute for the slender cypresses, J. virginiana 'Skyrocket' is a good choice. It can grow to 10 feet or more and will hardly be wider than 8 inches. Another good variety is J. v 'Grey Owl' of a colour indicated by the name. This variety is broad and bushy and flattens out at the top.

A good nursery catalogue often mentions more than fifty varieties worth having. They all grow well, even on poor soil, and need no pruning. Propagating is by cuttings, the species by seeds.

Juniperus squamata 'Meyeri'

JUNIPERUS (Juniper)

Among the great many plants that came to Europe in the nineteenth century was this green creeping conifer, J. squamata. It is native to the mountains of Nepal, where it grows up to the tree line of the Himalayas.

The original form is no longer sold but the variety H.s. 'Meyeri', introduced into this country in 1914, is one of the best conifers for the garden. It is a broad growing shrub with the bluest foliage of all junipers; the colour is most intense in vigorous shoots. Generally this variety is offered as a dwarf conifer, but in most gardens it will grow well over four feet, in particular on sandy soils. When the plant gets older, pruning may be necessary as it is liable to flop about.

Nurserymen are always looking for new varieties; they watch for the appearance of new forms and there are now a great many. One of these discoveries is the dwarf J.s. 'Blue Star' with fine blue-white foliage. Also J.s. 'Loderi', a slow growing conical form with blue-green leaves, is worth having. Both varieties will be welcome to the rockery and the small garden.

Junipers grow best in sandy soil. In a light place and protected against cold winds they will do well. They are hardly subject to any plant diseases and can be propagated by cuttings.

Juniperus chinensis 'Blaauw'   *J. pfitzeriana 'Aurea'*

JUNIPERUS (Juniper)

The number of colours, shades and habitats of Juniperus is endless. J. chinensis 'Blaauw' is a fine blue cultivar, beautiful in the rockery and grown in groups as a special feature. The first one was detected in a shipment of grafting stock and the name comes from the nursery in Boskoop, Holland where it was found.

The other illustrated plant is J. pfitzeriana 'Aurea', also very attractive with its golden foliage. It will be a success even in smaller gardens or at the edge of a pond. In spring and summer the young shoots are pure yellow, in winter they turn bronze. The original species, J. pfitzeriana, is bright green; a grey-green variety is J.p. 'Compacta', and a blue one J.p. 'Glauca'. All of them are not particular about the type of soil and need little care.

A slower grower is J. chinensis 'Plumosa Aurea', a good conifer for the smaller garden with bright yellow foliage in summer and a bronze green colour in winter. J.ch. 'Plumosa Aureovariegata' has golden yellow tips at the end of the short shoots.

Like other conifers, junipers should be used with some discretion. Their function is to form a background against which the drama of the summer garden is staged. Too many of them together take up too much room. However, they develop so pleasingly that it is difficult for a plant lover to discard any once they are growing well in a garden.

All varieties mentioned can be propagated by cuttings.

Kalmia latifolia

KALMIA (Calico bush)

K. latifolia is native to North America where it can reach a respectable height It is one of the most interesting evergreen shrubs available to the garden lover and it is the national flower of the State of New York. In May–June the shrub is covered with remarkable china-like flowers between white and red, and the stamens, standing out like ribs in an umbrella, enhance their appearance.

On account of its origin a calico bush is perfectly hardy, its only drawback being when the plant gets older it loses its leaves at the bottom and becomes leggy. Another small plant grown below it may cover this unattractive bareness.

Related is K. angustifolia; lower growing, less liable to loose leaves, and more profusely flowering, it will be preferred by many people. The variety 'Rubra' has carmine to dark red flowers.

Being woodland plants, kalmias like a moist soil and a somewhat shady position, though they can stand the sun. Therefore they do well together with rhododendrons, which enjoy the same soil conditions and provide the shade kalmias appreciate. A lime-free soil is essential. They are not very suitable for a small open garden. In moist soil runners are easily formed.

Pruning is not necessary. Propagation is possible by cuttings; with K. angustifolia the runners may be cut off and planted elsewhere.

Kerria japonica　　　　　　　*K. j. 'Pleniflora'*

KERRIA JAPONICA (Jew's mallow)

At the beginning of the nineteenth century a Mr William Kerr went to China on behalf of Kew Gardens. In 1804 he shipped a plant he had discovered to his principals and they honoured him by giving the plant his name: Kerria. Its flowers proved to be double. In 1834 another species with single flowers arrived; it is now known as K. japonica whereas the older one received the cultivar name 'Pleniflora'. Since then no new species or varieties have been discovered.

The double kerrias, broad shrubs, often man high, cheer up many of our gardens. In May–June appear double globular flowers in an orange-yellow colour. In winter the somewhat arching branches stay bright green. The single-flowered species is grown as well, and sometimes we find a variegated form under the name 'Picta', slower growing and with less flowers.

These excellent garden plants flourish in all kinds of soils and demand little attention. After flowering some old branches may be cut out to prevent the plant from becoming too crowded. Propagation is possible by cutting off the runners and by cuttings.

Kolkwitzia amabilis

KOLKWITZIA AMABILIS (Beauty bush)

It was only much later that it became clear how important was the discovery that plant explorers made when they brought Kolkwitzia from China to Europe about three-quarters of a century ago. Even now the shrub does not yet get the attention it deserves.

The many arching branches, with peeling brown bark, recall weigela, a close relative, but its form is more attractive. In larger gardens and parks we should see more of this fine shrub, but as it reaches a final height of some eight feet and spreads to the same extent, it is less suitable in a smaller garden.

The bell-shaped flowers appearing in May—June are pale pink and have yellow blotches on the inside. It flowers best in soil with only a little nitrogen that is not too fertile. The plant will flourish in the sun as well as in the shade.

When pruning it will be sufficient to take away old branches with little chance of flowering. After flowering younger branches may be cut away if that is necessary to keep its shape.

Propagation is possible by cuttings ; sometimes long branches will root spontaneously and can be cut from the mother plant.

Laburnum watereri 'Vossii'

LABURNUM (Golden rain)

The golden rain owes its revealing name and popularity to the beautiful hanging racemes that, together with the oval pinnate leaves, provide the golden beauty in May—June.

In a garden used by children or pets one should be aware that all parts of the plants are poisonous, in particular the seed pods appearing after the flowers. At any rate these should be gathered after flowering, a safety measure that moreover promotes the flowering in the next year.

Well-known golden rains are L. alpinum (Scotch laburnum) with longer racemes and smaller flowers than the original species, L. anagyroides (common laburnum) with shorter racemes flowering somewhat earlier than the other, and finally a cross between these two, L. watereri 'Vossii'. This is really the best one, with extra long racemes and slightly fragrant.

Fertile soil containing some lime is ideal for laburnums. A good position might be sunny or in half shade. Too moist a soil may have an unfavourable effect on flowering and might even prevent it completely.

An older shrub might have difficulty in getting re-established after transplanting but can revive even after several years. A young specimen needs some support till it is established.

Pruning is not necessary. Propagation of the species by seed ; varieties can be grafted.

Ligustrum ovalifolium 'Aureum'　　　　*Ligustrum vulgare*

LIGUSTRUM (Privet)

Of the many privet species the one originating from Japan—L. ovalifolium — is used most, in particular for hedges. People have planted miles of them, often without thinking of other, perhaps more attractive, hedging plants. Probably the property of losing the old leaves only when the new ones are already in sight made it so popular.

The plant is easy to cultivate and stands pruning very well; the leaves stay all winter except under conditions of severe frost. A nice variegated form is 'Aureum' with yellow blotched leaves liable to turn green in the shade. There are also silvery variegated forms with white-edged leaves.

L. vulgare is native of Europe; this strong grower is also suitable for hedging and, moreover, it is an attractive shrub, flowering for a long period with white panicles, followed by black berries in autumn. A wild hedge of this species can be very attractive.

A beautiful cross between L. ovalifolium 'Aureum' and L. vulgare is L. x vicary with yellow leaves turning greenish afterwards; it has a spreading habit and white flowers. Though this variety is suitable for hedging it does not stand pruning so very well.

A variety with very dark foliage is L.v. 'Viride'. Though brown in winter the leaves are not shed before spring. Somewhat less hardy is L. lucidum, resembling a miniature lilac with panicles of about 8 inches. This plant will be quite a success in a town garden.

Privets will grow everywhere, even in places where other plants barely survive. Hedges should be pruned at least twice a year, in spring and late summer. Propagation is by cuttings.

Liquidambar styraciflua

LIQUIDAMBAR STYRACIFLUA (Sweet gum)

At first sight this tree has much in common with a maple, chiefly on account of the palmate leaves, but in the case of the sweet gum they are arranged alternately on the branches—the leaves of maples are opposite each other—and give an unusual spicy odour when crushed. In its youth the plant bears remarkable corky wings on its branches and secretes an amber coloured resin that was once used medicinally.

In summer the foliage is bright green, but its unbelievable beauty comes in autumn when it is displaying all colours between yellow and blood red or even dark purple. The sweet gum is a real gem in the autumn garden and under ideal conditions will produce globular fruits at the same time.

The sweet gum is related to Hamamelis and came from America to Europe about three hundred years ago. The plant deserves everybody's attention; in moist soil that is reasonably fertile, and in an open, sunny position, it will prove a fast grower.

Though nowadays some landscape gardeners do not like exotics, it would be reasonable to make an exception of sweet gums, be it only on account of its marvellous colours. Moreover this plant is satisfied with any moist soil, is perfectly hardy and needs no pruning.

Propagation is possible by (imported) seeds. It is also worth noting that in America the wood is used for furniture under the name of red or yellow gum.

Lonicera periclymenum   *L. brownii 'Fuchsioides'*   *L. tellmanniana*

LONICERA (Honeysuckle)

The genus Lonicera has many exceptionally fine varieties that climb on pergolas and up buildings and even in hedges, where they draw attention by their richness of forms and colours. As soon as flowering starts moths and butterflies are attracted by the sweet scent of the nectar, especially in the evening. This scent even comes from cut flowers brought indoors.

Very attractive is L. brownii 'Fuchsioides' with leaves like saucers on which the red berries lie, just as on a green bowl. The flowers are orange and scarlet. Leaves and berries disappear after the first night frost.

A remarkable game of colours is played by L. periclymenum. Its flowers, which are also sweet scented in the evening, only last one day and within a few hours change colour from reddish through bright yellow to ocre; some days later they are followed by red berries. Bearing flowers and berries at the same time, the plant has an extraordinarily colourful appearance. Well known are the varieties known as Dutch honeysuckle, 'Belgica' and 'Serotina', the latter with narrow leaves.

A fast grower is L. tellmanniana with orange-yellow flowers in two parallel circles appearing in May–June. When young the foliage has an olive colour, afterwards turning green with a dewy underside.

Most honeysuckles are satisfied with any good soil and flower in a sunny as well as in a shaded place. Pruning is necessary to keep the plant within reasonable bounds; sometimes it may be cut back to the old wood. Propagation from cuttings is simple.

Lonicera tatarica

Lonicera pileata

LONICERA

There are many shrubbery species and varieties. L. tatarica is a native of the Asiatic steppes and as a consequence is very hardy.

It is not a plant suited to the small garden; it needs some room. It can be used to hide a wall or a shed and may form the background to lower planting. It is advisable not to plant it too close to a path, as after rain the branches are liable to bend under the weight of the water and can surprise a passer by with an unexpected shower.

The shrub starts growing very early in the season, often in autumn, but the green shoots will hardly be damaged by frost or snow. The many white to pinkish flowers bloom in May—June, somewhat later than the leaves. By July—August the first red berries appear as the harbingers of autumn.

Attractive varieties are the white 'Alba' and the low growing deep pink 'Zabelli'. Of a quite different appearance is L. pileata, a low spreading evergreen bush covering walls as well as the ground, with inconspicuous flowers but violet berries in autumn.

Loniceras do not demand much from the soil. In exposed places the evergreen varieties might be damaged slightly during winter but recover fast. Pruning can be limited to rejuvenating and shaping the shrubs. Propagating by cuttings is possible.

Magnolia stellata

Magnolia liliflora 'Nigra'

MAGNOLIA

As soon as we get the first warm weather of spring (though often a late snow shower warns us that winter is not entirely over), the flowers in the remarkable hairy buds of several Magnolia varieties are ready to unfold. When Forsythia has given the signal for an early spring Magnolia will follow shortly afterwards.

The first to flower is M. stellata, the star magnolia, unfolding its large star-like flowers on a shrub that reaches a height of about 10 feet after many years. Of the same size is M. liliflora 'Nigra' (known for years as M. soulangeana 'Nigra') but its flowers, liable to be damaged by late frosts, appear somewhat later. The flowers have something in common with big purple tulips and as a consequence the plant has been wrongly called tulip tree (the true tulip tree is, in fact, Liriodendron). The flowers are still on the shrub when the leaves have unfolded and sometimes a second flowering may follow, but the greater part is then hidden by the summer leaves.

This beautiful shrub may grow to a small tree but this takes such a long time it can safely be planted in a small garden. Most magnolias, particularly the early flowering kinds, need a sheltered position away from cold winds, and the majority do not like lime and prefer good rich soil. Planting is best done in February. The root ball must not be damaged.

Pruning should be restricted to the removal of dead branches only. Propagation is by layering and cuttings.

Mahonia aquifolium

MAHONIA AQUIFOLIUM (Oregon grape)

As with other plants, the name of the species reveals that this Oregon grape was one of the plants with spiny leaves – just like hollies, barberries, Osmanthus and even some oaks, originally grouped together under the name of Aquifolium.

The leaves, composed of five to nine spiny toothed leaflets, help to create variation of colour in the garden : immediately after the appearance of the bright yellow flowers, and at the same time as bulbs are flowering, the reddish-yellow spring shoots appear, providing a lively contrast to the dark older foliage, which in most winters survives without damage but turns beautifully purple or bronze green in the mean time. The dark blue berries often stay on the shrub until the following spring.

Mahonias will not grow much over three feet, so the height will seldom be a problem, unlike the runners which root easily and may be cut off with a spade. Other pruning can be limited to removing old branches. The soil is hardly important and the place can be shady, even under trees. The winter foliage is often used in flower arrangements.

Seedlings are extremely variable and of course nurserymen have made use of this property and have selected new varieties, e.g. 'Atropurpurea' with very dark foliage. M. bealei has strong pinnate leaves, their green contrasting nicely with the upright yellow racemes, appearing in April–May. M. japonica has a sturdier growth and large green leaves, often hiding the flowers that appear very early, sometimes even in February. It differs from M. bealei in that it has drooping flower sprays. Propagation is possible from seeds, but also from cuttings and by transplanting of rooted runners.

Malus 'Lemoinei'

Malus 'Red Siberian'

MALUS (Crab apple)

In spring, especially in May, the ornamental crab apples make a magnificent display. During the remainder of the year they are rather inconspicuous, though some varieties have fine dark red foliage and beautiful fruits in autumn. Still they attract attention during their flowering period, their branches thickly covered with blossoms in colours between white and dark red.

There are so many that it is difficult for the garden lover to make a choice. This short summary might be a help.

Most crab apples are varieties of M. baccata or M. floribunda and their hybrids. Worth while are M. coronaria 'Charlottae' with large light pink flowers, M. sargentii (white flowers, pink buds) M. 'Aldenhamensis' (red flowers, brown fruits), M. 'Almey' (red flowers, orange-red fruits), M. 'Eleyi' (wine red flowers, darker fruits), M. 'Hopa' (purple red flowers, bright red fruits), M. 'John Downie' (white flowers, orange-red fruits), M. 'Lemoinei' (deep crimson flowers, dark purple fruits), M. 'Liset', (red flowers, black fruits), M. 'Red Siberian' (white flowers, yellow, red blushing fruits) and M. 'Van Eseltine' (pink double flowers, yellowish green fruits).

Crab apples do not ask much from the soil but they are ideal to grow on chalk. The sunnier the position the better will they flower. Real pruning is not necessary, but in February old branches or those spoiling the shape of the plant can be cut. Skilful pruning makes it possible to form a standard out of a shrub; some varieties are sold grafted as standards. Propagation is by grafting.

Metasequoia glyptostroboides

METASEQUOIA GLYPTOSTROBOIDES (Dawn redwood)

To garden lovers searching for a particular tree as a conversation piece this dawn redwood is recommended. It is one of the latest discoveries in the plant world: it was not before 1945 that three specimens were discovered in Szechwan, China, and in 1947 the first seeds came to the western world. Already trees of up to 45 feet have been grown in many countries and it has been found to be a fast grower. Later, just before travelling to China was prohibited (even to plant explorers), more than a thousand dawn redwoods were seen there, some of them of a size of over a hundred feet. It is now generally believed that it has commercial possibilities as well as ornamental value.

The beauty of the tree, which is similar to Taxodium, lies in its fine conical shape. Furthermore it is very hardy and easy to grow. The price is reasonable so would make an attractive feature in a somewhat large garden. It appreciates damp soil close to water, and as its natural rate of growth is about three feet in one season the plant will soon reach a considerable height.

Pruning is not normally necessary, but cold winter winds might dry out the top shoot and then a new top should be created by cutting competing branches in order to enable the strongest remaining shoot to develop.

Propagation by cuttings is easy.

Osmanthus ilicifolius

OSMANTHUS ILICIFOLIUS

This plant, which is also sold as O. heterophyllus, is a lesson in botanical observance, as it can very easily be mistaken for holly. As a matter of fact in the past it was grouped together with holly and other spiny leaved plants under the genus Aquifolium.

A distinct difference is the position of the leaves: they are not alternate, as with holly, but are arranged in opposite pairs. A similarity is that the leaves of both genera are leathery and stay on the plant during winter. Nevertheless the variation is considerable, some leaves being prickly and holly-like, while others, often on the same plant, are ovate and only spine-tipped. It flowers in summer; the small, tubular, strongly scented flowers are borne in dense axillary clusters along the branches. Their fragrance attracts bees and other insects.

The shrub does not grow very fast and will finally reach a height of about seven feet. It can be used as a hedging plant as well as a solitary specimen. It is even possible to clip it in shapes such as a cone or an obelisk.

A native of the woods of Japan and China, the plant prefers a half-shady position. If the plant is damaged in a severe winter this is due to drying winds rather than to the cold. The variegated form is very rare.

Propagation is possible by grafting on Ligustrum vulgare or L. ovalifolium, pointing to a close relation between the genera. Cuttings can be used as well as seeds, which should be sown in a greenhouse immediately after ripening.

Pachysandra terminalis

PACHYSANDRA TERMINALIS

No doubt this is one of the best groundcover plants, a remarkably strong, nearly indestructible woody shrub and a close relative of the boxwood, generally used for hedging.

In places where grass cannot grow due to lack of light, for instance in the shade of trees, Pachysandra is a good substitute. Planting twelve of them to a square yard will be sufficient; with their underground runners spreading in all directions the plants weave a carpet too thick to be penetrated by any weed. From time to time a little soil with humus should be scattered among the plants to keep them in good trim.

The leathery foliage of Pachysandra, native of Japan and China, is a distinct advantage; it will not be affected by water dripping from the trees or by old leaves falling. The small shrubs, not higher than eight inches, flower in March—April; the white soft scented flowers have prominent white stamens with brown tips that make them visible but the white berries that follow are not conspicuous.

The plant is very hardy, though the foliage may change colour due to frost. A variegated form has the same qualities as the green one.

Pruning may be limited to trimming the runners. Propagation is easy by transplanting rooted runners.

Parthenocissus

PARTHENOCISSUS (Virginia creeper)

The name of this well-known climbing plant has been changed by botanists recently, but to many people the name is still Ampelopsis. Nevertheless the official name is Parthenocissus and the best known variety is the illustrated P. quinquefolia, no doubt the most clinging of all climbers. Unfortunately, this true Virginia Creeper is often confused with P. tricuspidata which is correctly called Boston Ivy. The palmate discs can even adhere to glass, marble and other smooth surfaces. As a consequence the thick layer of foliage can reach the unbelievable height of about 50 feet and even more, thus completely covering buildings, chimneys and towers with its usually three-lobed leaves, turning vivid shades of red in autumn. Nowadays it is particularly appreciated that the plant is very resistant to air pollution, heat and smoke, and will grow on industrial sites as well as in the country.

The Virginia creeper will feel at home in any soil as long as the base can be kept reasonably cool; the shoots will reach for the sun. Pruning is extremely simple: the plant may be cut back as far as necessary and will always recover within a short time.

Propagation may be done by cuttings and grafting. To those interested in making experiments, sowing seed is worth trying. Afterwards a selection of the best forms can be made.

Passiflora caerulea

PASSIFLORA CAERULEA (Passion flower)

To some readers it may be a surprise to find the passion flower in this shrub book, as the plant is also sold as a pot plant for indoors. As a matter of fact the passion flower lives on the border line between living room and the garden. In colder winters and in exposed places it is not completely hardy, but against the southern wall of a house, and provided the base is covered in cold periods, it has a good chance of survival.

Even after winter damage, the plant will quickly make shoots of up to 12 feet in spring. They will grab any support they meet on their way up. From June to September numerous flowers, lasting only 24 hours, will appear. These unusual flowers made a deep impression on the plant explorers who first discovered them in Brazil. In the stamens and stalked ovary they saw the symbols of the Passion, hence the name.

Perhaps it is useful to repeat that the plant needs a southern position. Ordinary soil is satisfactory; in rich ground the plant makes strong growth at the expense of the flowers. The plant's enemy is drought and therefore it should be watered in May—June if rain is scarce. If a plant grows too strongly, producing few flowers, confine the roots to a brick-lined bed; this will slow up the rate of growth.

Besides the original species there is a well-known variety 'Constance Elliott' with nearly white flowers — those of the species are bluish — but the same general properties.

Propagation is possible by cuttings or layering the shoots. A passion flower kept as a pot plant indoors may be cut back and put into the garden in spring. It is necessary to remove the pot and to water the root ball thoroughly.

102

Pernettya mucronata

PERNETTYA MUCRONATA

This remarkable plant comes from South America and is a native of the Andes mountains, brought to Western Europe only a century ago.

In autumn Pernettya is often sold as a pot plant or as part of a flower arrangement; it is also the time to buy it at garden centres. Plant lovers are fond of the white, pink or red berries which look well together with yellow conifers, as shown in the photograph.

Being a unisexual plant the females will only give berries if there is a male in the neighbourhood. At the start of summer the bees take care of the pollination. Should no male—which is somewhat looser growing—specimen be available, the female plant is only a very ordinary shrub with spiny leaves and without any appeal. There are, however, hermaphrodite forms, such as Bell's Seedling.

The original plant arrived in Europe with small purple berries, but by crossing and selection nurserymen created a number of fine varieties, many of them named. A well-known one is 'Wintertime' with white berries lasting nearly to Christmas.

In loose peaty soil runners are formed that may be used for propagation, but preference should be given to cuttings and seedlings from which selection of the finest varieties, and of course also male plants, is possible. It is interesting to note that thrushes did not take the berries at first, but after some generations they developed a taste for them. The fruit is also eaten by ground birds in the winter.

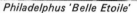
Philadelphus 'Belle Etoile' *P. coronarius* *P. 'Virginal'*

PHILADELPHUS (Mock orange)

In the early summer the mock orange is one of the most important flowering garden shrubs. After a hesitating start, generally in May, the principal flowering period will last the whole month of June and even part of July. The folwers are always white, though the variety 'Belle Etoile' has a little purple in the heart.

Philadelphus coronarius is a low dense shrub with creamy white flowers appearing at the end of May and with a scent like oranges. The variety 'Aureus' is grown for its striking golden foliage which gradually turns green later in the summer.

A large variation may be found among the hybrids, the best known of which are the earlier named 'Belle Etoile' and the sweet scented 'Albâtre'. Owners of small gardens will be pleased with 'Manteau d'Hermine' with a low growth and flowers having a tendency to be double. A strong grower is 'Virginal', easily reaching seven feet with fragrant flowers of which the greater part will be double; flowering branches may be kept in water for several days. A tall shrub is 'Voie Lactée' with large single flowers without scent but with a golden glow caused by long yellow stamens.

A mock orange will grow in any reasonable soil and will like a sunny place. As the flowers bloom on branches of the previous year the shrub should never be pruned in spring. After the flowering period branches that are too straggly may be cut back.

Propagation by cuttings is not difficult.

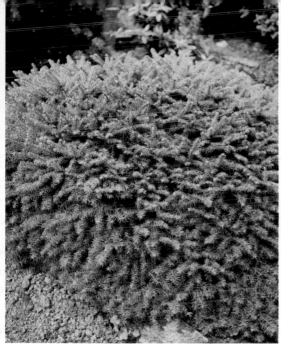

Picea abies 'Nidiformis'   *P. omorika*

PICEA (Spruce or fir)

Most Christmas trees are seedlings of the European fir – Picea abies – that covers large areas in Europe and is one of the most important suppliers of timber. In addition to that, the genus is botanically interesting, especially on account of its numerous dwarf forms of which the illustrated P.a. 'Nidiformis', with its broad conical growth, is one of the finest. This dwarf is very suitable for a rock garden, just like many others. A choice will be difficult and therefore the best thing to be done is look round a nursery or garden centre in order to compare a number of dwarf spruces. Good varieties are 'Compacta', 'Gregoryana', 'Gregoryana Veitchii', 'Ohlendorffii', 'Pygmaea', 'Maxwellii', 'Procumbens', 'Pumila Nigra' and 'Repens'.

Dwarf spruces grow in any good garden soil and prefer full light; under trees they do not do well.

The second illustration shows a Serbian spruce – P. omorika – a conifer that will grow well even under adverse conditions, e.g. in polluted air. The bark is orange brown, and the needles are dark green with two white bands beneath. The form being variable, it is worth while selecting a plant with a nice conical shape.

Dwarf spruces are propagated by cuttings or grafting, but P. omorika is grown from seeds. Branches reverting to the wild spruce form and thus spoiling the dwarf growth should be cut, but further pruning may be limited to the removal of old branches. With conicals it is important to keep one top branch.

Picea glauca 'Conica'   *P. pungens 'Glauca'*   *P. p. 'Glauca Kosteri'*

PICEA (Spruce or fir)

Only a short time ago Picea glauca 'Conica' was known as P. albertiana 'Conica' and the old name had the advantage of revealing something about its origin. As a matter of fact it is a dwarf form of Canada's native spruce, in particular growing in the western province of Alberta and generally known as 'white spruce'.

A blue variety, discovered somewhat later, is P. glauca 'Conica' (illustrated left), a cone form with dense foliage that found its way over the whole world after its chance discovery in 1904. It is suitable for small gardens and may reach a size of about four feet, provided the conditions are favourable. It may be used in rockeries and as a winter planting outside in containers; in exposed positions the needles tend to turn brown.

An entirely different plant is P. pungens, imported from the United States more than a century ago and known as Colorado blue spruce. Seedlings of this species may vary from green to light blue. Dutch nurserymen have given much attention to the selection and propagation; their names may be found in those of fine varieties like 'Moerheimii', 'Kosteri', 'Spekii', 'Endtzii' and 'Vuykii'. In particular 'Kosteri' is well known and is in strong demand for its silvery-white shoots, first limp, later rigid, turning to a fine shade of blue. It is an ideal tree for the centre of a lawn, but rather expensive due to the work involved in propagation, but it is indeed a tree for a lifetime.

Pruning is limited to the occasional removal of a "wild" shoot. Any garden soil is acceptable. Propagation demands professional skill; it is done by grafting on a wild spruce.

Pieris japonica

P. floribunda

PIERIS (Andromeda)

Coming from the Far East, the best known type is P. japonica, still popular under its old name Andromeda japonica; another is P. floribunda.

P. japonica is an evergreen flowering shrub with a spread of 6–10 feet and a height of 7 feet. The oblong ovate leaves display a fine copper colour in spring that turns shiny bright green in summer. In March–April the flowers appear in pendulant clusters (similar to lily of the valley) that can be seen as reddish buds in winter. P. floribunda grows somewhat faster and flowers in April–May, but in erect terminal panicles; moreover the foliage is somewhat brighter green than that of P. japonica.

A welcome quality of both shrubs is their green foliage in winter, especially important in smaller gardens. The best soil is humus peat of the same type used for rhododendrons and azaleas. Care should be taken that the root ball does not dry out during transplanting. A little peat moss at the base may assist the growth that will, moreover, benefit from a shady position. There are now several named varieties, including P. formosa 'forrestii', which has startling bright red young foliage that gradually turns green by the summer. Forest Flame, another variety, also has red young leaves.

Pruning only means removing old flowers and trimming young shoots growing in the wrong direction. Propagation is possible by seeds and cuttings.

Pinus mugo 'Mughus'

Pinus pumila

PINUS (Pine)

The pine, in particular the Scotch pine – Pinus sylvestris – is the best-known forest tree all over Western Europe but is not a real garden plant. For that purpose Pinus mugo, the mountain pine from Central and South Eastern Europe, is more valuable. Generally it is a shrub-form with a somewhat gnarled appearance, but as the plant is very variable it is difficult to find two seedlings looking exactly alike.

In gardens and rockeries P.m. 'Mughus' and its interesting dwarf forms are used, all with their mid-green needles in pairs, a property that makes pines easily distinguishable from spruces and firs.

In rockeries and smaller gardens P. pumila, with needles in groups of five, is a good choice. The illustration shows it in a group planting mixed with bulbs. The best-known variety is P. pumila 'Glauca' with bluish grey needles. These pines, accustomed as they are to the bright light of the high mountains, prefer a light place in the garden. They may be used everywhere, even in poor sandy soil.

Propagation is done by grafting named varieties on seedling root stocks—a job for a specialist.

Special attention should be drawn to P. sylvestris 'Watereri', a globular shrub with conspicuous blue-grey needles. It was found on Horsell Common, near Woking in Surrey, by Mr. Anthony Waterer.

Polygonum baldschuanicum

POLYGONUM BALDSCHUANICUM (Russian vine)

The variety of forms even within one genus is often unbelievable. This might be said about the genus Polygonum, containing water and swamp plants, such as P. amphibium, as well as climbers, among which is P. baldschuanicum. This super climber was brought from Russia to Europe less than a century ago and will easily grow 30–45 feet in one summer. This makes the plant useful in hiding unsightly buildings, as it always manages to find a support to grow higher. With the help of chicken wire it is even possible to use a Russian vine as a hedge plant, e.g. to surround large unsightly areas.

In the summer of the second year after planting the flowers will appear, generally for the first time in July and afterwards again in September/October, often lasting until the first frost. The white or pale pink flowers are borne in panicles of about 10–18 inches in length.

If the plant is climbing against a living tree the latter may run the risk of being choked completely.

The Russian vine will grow anywhere provided the soil is moist enough and the position a little shaded. Hard pruning right down to the ground may be necessary and in order to prevent the plant from taking over the garden and even the house it can be cut back to half-size every spring; within a short time it will reach its original height again.

propagation is possible by cuttings or grafting on its own roots.

Potentilla fruticosa 'Jackman's Variety'   *P. fr. 'Farreri'*

POTENTILLA (Shrubby cinquefoil)

Potentillas start flowering when many of the well-known garden shrubs have already passed their climax. Nevertheless they are among the longest flowering plants of the garden, as from June to October they keep unfolding their numerous yellow or white flowers.

The varieties vary in habit and P. arbuscula is a semi-prostrate plant with large bright yellow flowers that may be used as a ground cover. 'Jackman's Variety' is a rather tall shrub with dark leaves and still larger yellow flowers, highly recommended as a solitary specimen. A lower plant is P. fruticosa 'Farreri' with smaller flowers. 'Maanelys' blooms twice with lemon coloured flowers and is a suitable dwarf hedging plant.

A really useful ground cover plant is 'Mandschurica' with semi-prostrate blue-green foliage and numerous white flowers. A recent variety is 'Abbotswood', rather low and with a spreading growth; the flowers are white and large.

With the help of different varities it is possible to build up an attractive collection, even in smaller gardens. A sunny position is important as potentillas are real lovers of the sun and more sun means more flowers. The plant will grow in half shade, but that restricts its flowering.

Pruning can be limited to cutting away old branches and weak shoots. Propagation is by cuttings; varieties will not be true to their original beauty from seed.

Prunus 'Kiku-shidare-sakura'

P. triloba 'Plena'

'P. Kanzan'

PRUNUS (Ornamental cherry, plum or almond)

Many shrubs and trees which flower abundantly in spring belong to this genus, which includes ornamental plums, peaches, cherries and almonds. It is only a pity that the flowers are often damaged prematurely by bleak spring winds.

The Japanese have created many beautiful varieties, in particular P. serrulata, flowering in April–May, such as P.s. 'Amanogawa' with soft pink flowers, which, on account of its nearly erect branches, is extremely suitable to the small garden. 'Kiku-shidare-sakura' is a beautiful weeping tree with double deep pink flowers, often flowering in April. 'Kanzan', with its fine clusters of dark pink flowers, is extremely popular.

Owners of smaller gardens will be pleased with the illustrated P. triloba 'Plena'. The flowers, which resemble miniature roses, stand on very short stems along the branches, smothering them from sight almost completely in March and April. This variety, which is often cultivated as a standard, should be pruned in order to stimulate flowering. In early summer the branches should be cut back close to their base as the new stems produce the branches that will flower next year. Older, regularly pruned shrubs look more or less like old pollarded willows. Other species should not be pruned.

A fine plant is the dark leaved P. cerasifera 'Nigra', still generally known as P. pissardii; the pink or white flowers appear in spring. In autumn, and often again in early spring, P. subhirtella 'Autumnalis' unfolds its white or pink flowers. This is a valuable shrub for those trying to produce flowers in their garden every day of the year.

Propagating is possible by cuttings and grafting.

Prunus laurocerasus 'Otto Luyken'

PRUNUS LAUROCERASUS (Cherry laurel)

For centuries this plant, brought to western Europe from the Balkans, has been used for its medicinal qualities as the older name, Laurocerasus officinalis, indicates.

Though apparently an outsider in the genus Prunus, the species is a worthy member of the family. In winter it enlivens the garden with its long evergreen leaves; in spring the white flowers, borne in axillary and terminal racemes, come as a real surprise. Thanks to hybrids created by nurserymen, there are very fine varities now. 'Caucasica' is a fast growing type which flowers abundantly with white racemes. Very hardy and wind resistant, too, is 'Otto Luyken'. The dull green 'Reynvaanii', with conspicuous large leaves, is a slow growing form. Those looking for a spreading, but still not too tall a shrub, may be happy with 'Schipkaensis' with its upright racemes. Still finer is the improved variety 'Macrophylla' with extraordinarily profuse flowering.

Alkaline soils are unsuitable for cherry laurels. They are useful when young as tub or container plants. Older ones can be pruned in March–April at the time when the buds are developing. Care should be taken that flower buds and large leaves are undamaged and therefore a knife is safer than pruning shears.

Propagation by cuttings.

Pyracantha 'Orange Charmer'

PYRACANTHA (Firethorn)

The firethorn was described as early as 1629. The species comes from south eastern Europe and West Asia, but the present garden varieties are comparatively new plants. Fine coloured pictures in catalogues have stimulated sales tremendously.

In May the firethorn unfolds its hawthorn-like florets in large clusters and attracts many bees and early butterflies. When late in autumn and in winter nearly all berried plants are stripped by birds and frosts the colourful berries of the firethorn are still there, together with the evergreen leaves. Birds only touch them if nothing else can be found.

The best position is against a wall where the plant reaches a considerable height. They can also be used as hedging plants but during the essential pruning the greater part of the flower buds will be cut off and as a consequence only few berries can be expected.

Modern varieties, such as 'Golden Charmer' with orange-yellow berries, 'Orange Charmer' with deep orange, and 'Orange Glow' with still more orange-red fruits, have proved to be resistant to disease.

Firethorns are raised in pots and delivered that way. When planted the root ball should be handled with care and the soil should not contain any lime; applying peat moss to the soil is helpful. If in spring the plant appears damaged by winter weather it may have been too dry and should be watered; protection against strong spring sunshine is advisable.

Pruning should be limited to cutting away old wood, remembering that the flowers will appear on the branches made in the previous year. Propagation is by cuttings.

R. 'Caractacus'   *R. 'Van Weerden Poelman'*

RHODODRENDON

Here we have a remarkable group of plants, most of them resulting from complicated hybridisation, sometimes with parents from two, or even three, continents: America, Asia and Europe. Hybridizing still continues; one of the nurserymen's cherished dreams is a good yellow variety, hardy on the European continent. The prospects are better than in the past as nowadays the pollen can be stored in deep freeze and such techniques as the use of radiation with gamma rays have produced surprising results.

A healthy rhododendron hybrid has dark green leathery leaves, staying on the plant for years. Even after half a century the plant can still be dense and green, showing thick flower buds every autumn that will open in May for a comparatively short, but beautiful, flowering period.

Important is the right soil: rhododendrons like humus and hate lime and it is recommended to make a large planting hole and fill it with peat moss before planting. The root balls should be soaked well; standing in water overnight before planting will be beneficial.

In spite of their leathery foliage, rhododendrons need a moist position and should be watered after planting and in a dry summer. Pruning is never needed; old leggy plants may be sawn off close to the ground and buds that have been dormant for years will appear and give the plant its original size within a short time. On account of the fibrous root ball transplanting is easy.

Propagation is by cuttings and grafting.

Rhododendron 'Elizabeth'   *R. 'Blue Tit'*

RHODODENDRON

The well-known large flowering rhododendrons command general admiration, but, needing much room, they may crowd even a large garden, especially if used in a group. Hardly anybody has enough courage to remove such fine old plants.

Nurserymen, always seeking novelties, concentrate on producing varieties of a smaller size as these, according to experts, have a great future. In particular the repens hybrids, grown by the German Mr. Hobbie, are a real advance. They all have a prostrate growth and are strongly branched. On the terminal of their shoots there are two to three more or less bell-shaped flowers, often in striking colours.

These rhododenrons, giving pleasure in small as well as in large gardens, are very hardy and wind resistant. Good examples are 'Baden-Baden' (brilliant red and rich flowering), 'Carmen' (red with dark shade, prostrate plant), 'Elisabeth Hobbie' (blood red), 'Elizabeth' (dark red), and 'Scarlet Wonder' (brilliant red, very prolific).

Especially suitable to the small garden, and in strong demand, are the blue flowering dwarf varieties with small leaves. They succeed almost anywhere if the plant hole is filled with peat moss before planting. Their flowering period is long and often commences at the beginning of April; late frosts may nip the flowers.

Recommended varieties are 'Blue Diamond' (bright purplish blue—25 inches), 'Blue Tit' (light lavender—25 inches), 'Oudijk's Favourite' (purplish blue—15 inches), and 'Moerheim' (light purple—12 inches).

Rhododendron praecox

Rhododendron 'Catawbiense grandiflorum' (page 114

RHODODENDRON

Besides the well-known rhododendron hybrids, often the results of complicated crosses and with ancestors that have dropped back into oblivion, there are also rhododendrons with pure blood that have come to our gardens straight from nature. These are really in the right place when used in heather gardens. Even if they do not have the large flowers and the dazzling beauty of the hybrids, they have special charms for plant lovers.

Very popular is the fine purple blue R. praecox, often flowering as early as the first of March. If night frosts are not too severe the flowers remain undamaged and their beauty can last a whole month. Ideal for the rockery is the low growing R. impeditum (height 6–14 inches, spread up to 24 inches), which originates from China, with pale mauve to purplish blue funnel-shaped flowers.

A real alpine rhododendron is R. hirsutum, unfolding its rose-pink flowers in June. This variety can stand some lime in the soil, just as R. ferrugineum, a variable species; its dark pink to dark red flowers may be expected in June. In the alpine areas on the Continent wild rhododendrons are protected plants; digging them up is strictly forbidden.

In larger gardens and in background planting R. ponticum, normally used as understock for grafting, will be quite a success. It will reach a height of many feet and the flowers, light purple with a yellow or orange blotch, appear in May–June.

All plants described, except R. praecox, need soil with humus but without lime. If necessary peat moss in the planting hole will be helpful. Propagation is by seeds—again except R. praecox—but that takes much time and careful nursing.

Rhus typhina

RHUS TYPHINA (Stag's-horn sumach)

This sumach originated from the eastern United States and is much favoured by modern garden architects. With a height of 10–15 feet and many main stems branching close to the ground, it is a highly decorative plant. The soft hairy shoots are brown and always feel warm. When in spring the pinnate leaves, up to 18 inches long, have unfolded, the plant has a more or less tropical character. The female specimens have long, remarkably red, clusters in autumn, giving the tree or shrub—depending on the way it is pruned—an exotic appearance; they stay on the branches till spring. In autumn the foliage takes on brilliant colours. In particular the variety 'Laciniata', with finely cut leaves, is very decorative.

It is remarkable that in America R. typhina is a bothersome weed. It grows in any soil and as it does not mind lime it is extremely suitable for building sites.

Some people may be allergic to the plant; all parts are more or less poisonous and families with children should be cautious. The plants produce underground runners that shoot up all over the garden, but perhaps friends may be delighted to have them as they propagate easily by this means. Sumachs growing strongly can stand hard pruning of the stems and new shoots will soon develop.

Ribes sanguineum 'King Edward VII'

RIBES SANGUINEUM (Flowering currant)

The flowering currant is closely related to the common currant which its leaves closely resemble. Its early flowering habit makes it a welcome feature in the spring garden. The soft green leaves are only half unfolded when the fine pendant racemes, often over four inches long, show their light to dark pink colour.

The variety 'King Edward VII' has very large crimson flowers; 'Grandiflorum'—as the name implies—has large bright red blooms; and the flowers of 'Pulborough Scarlet' have a little white in their hearts.

Flowering currants can be used as solitary specimens but also mix with other later flowering shrubs; together they may eventually form a loose hedge. The bushes grow fast and may reach 7 feet or more and in the meantime they will spread as well. In autumn the blue-black berries appear, but they have hardly any decorative value.

Any soil is acceptable but the plant does not like shade. Pruning should be done sparingly and limited to removing shoots with little chance of flowering and thinning the stems after flowering.

Propagating is easy by hardwood cuttings in October.

Robinia hispida

ROBINIA HISPIDA (Rose acacia)

Most robinias or acacias are trees; still there are some exceptions, among which is Robinia hispida (popularly named rose acacia) being a shrub with brittle shoots and many root runners. The former quality prevents the plant from reaching full development in windy positions and in places with much snow or where the shrub can be easily damaged by playing children.

The branches are covered with red bristles and bear pinnate leaves. In May–June, and in some favourable summers again in August, the pendant racemes of rose-pink flowers appear, in shape and size more or less looking like those of the sweet pea. To us they are not fragrant but nevertheless they attract many bees with their abundant nectar. During the flowering period the branches often bend under their flowering burden.

R. kelseyi has much in common with R. hispida—its prickly stems are just as brittle and therefore the plant is often grafted on a main stem of false acacia, making it less vulnerable. The flowers are smaller than with R. hispida.

Robinias prefer good, if possible lime containing, garden soil and like a sunny position. When the plant is still young the forming of new branches may be stimulated by pruning; in this way their brittleness will be of less concern.

Propagation is simple; the runners can be dug up and planted elsewhere. People wanting a standard rather than a shrub can graft R. hispida on a stem of the false acacia R. pseudoacacia, as shown above.

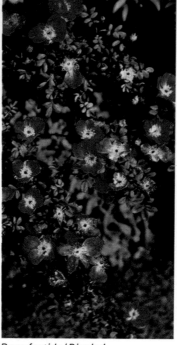

Rosa hugonis   *Rosa foetida 'Bicolor'*   *Rosa rugosa 'Hansa'*

ROSA

At the end of the last century the culture of roses was already highly developed as many growers had been occupying themselves with complicated hybridising; hundreds of superb double varieties were the result.

In 1899 Kew Gardens received rose seeds from China collected by a missionary. It came from a strong shrub growing up to seven feet with beautiful yellow flowers, unfolding so early—sometimes a month before other roses—that it is a real spring flowering shrub. This rose was named R. hugonis, after Father Hugo.

The flowering on the branches of the previous year implies that the shrub should not be pruned, only thinned from time to time. This rose will grow on any soil and may be used as a garden divider, though it will not make a formal hedge. Its hips are black-red.

The second rose illustrated here is officially named R. foetida 'Bicolor' but has been popularly known as 'Austrian Copper' for a long time. The scientific name reveals that the flowers have two colours: the crown is orange on the inside and yellow on the outside. This rose was recorded in the sixteenth century. Its size never being more than 6 feet, it is suitable for smaller gardens. As with all roses of this type, the flowers appear on the old wood and therefore pruning should be limited to essential thinning only. The flowering period is short: it lasts from the middle to the end of June, but then the fine foliage on arching branches remains. In general hips are rarely seen.

An advantage of this rose is its survival in dark places where other botanica. roses will hardly keep alive.

Rosa rugosa

Rosa moyesii

ROSA

It was only at the beginning of this century that Rosa moyesii came to Western Europe. Its cradle was in China where it grows wild as a sturdy plant with wine red single flowers displaying conspicuous yellow stamens, a rare combination in roses. The orange-red hips are pear-shaped.

If the shade is not too deep the shrub may be grown under trees, but as the plant will not accept much interference pruning should only be done with great care. Fine varieties are 'Geranium' with flaming red flowers and orange hips, 'Sealing Wax' with purplish pink flowers and sealing wax red hips, and 'Fargesii' with pink flowers and red hips. Among the hybrids, 'Nevada' is favourite on account of its large white flowers.

The other rose illustrated is R. rugosa, the Japanese briar, which was introduced into Europe in 1796 but even at that time was the parent of many oriental varieties in its native country. It is reasonably resistance to air pollution and sea winds, and is also suitable as a hedge plant.

The shrubs require little attention. Their flowering period is towards the end of May, but they generally produce a number of odd flowers in summer; they are followed by a profusion of orange-red hips. Outstanding varieties are white 'Alba' and purplish red 'Rubra'. Hybridisation has produced the red double flowered 'F. J. Grootendorst' and pink 'Pink Grootendorst'. The fragrant double red 'Hansa' (page 120) is certainly worth while, as is also the old-timer (dating back to 1892) 'Blanc Double de Coubert'.

Propagation is by cuttings and grafting.

121

Rosa omeiensis 'Pteracantha'

ROSA OMEIENSIS

From olden times people have had a preference for odd plants, variegated colours and strange forms, and this has kept the growers busy for centuries; there is always a strong demand for something new and different. In this way the assortment of ornamental plants has become very large and nurserymen all over the world have contributed, the British and the Dutch being foremost.

Without making a garden into a museum of oddities it may be attractive to have some rare plants as conversation pieces. Those who are interested should look for the remarkable Rosa omeiensis 'Pteracantha', which, like many other roses, is a native of China. Most conspicuous are the fern-like leaves; the plant may be used as a solitary specimen or in groups, especially in a more or less informal garden.

Hardly any other species has so long a flowering period; it starts around the end of May and the flowers, generally with four white petals, are quickly followed by large numbers of pear-shaped hips on swollen stalks.

The illustrated 'Pteracantha' is sometimes called "barbed wire rose" on account of its large thorns, translucent and blood red, especially on young shoots—a beautiful sight in low winter sunshine. Older shrubs have darker, more opaque thorns.

Hard pruning promotes the growth of young shoots covered with bright red thorns. The plant may be used for hedging, but if children are around the thorns are too dangerous.

This rose makes no demands on soil or position. Propagation is by grafting on wild understock.

Salix matsudana 'Tortuosa'

SALIX MATSUDANA 'TORTUOSA' (Corkscrew willow)

Many plant lovers admire a plant for its fine foliage, its beautiful flowers or its general appearance in summer, but some, in addition, appreciate its silhouette in winter. To them the corkscrew willow is a special joy as its branches are twisted in a remarkable way.

In summer dress this willow is hardly different from other members of the family but when the leaves are shed the crazy pattern of the twisted shoots and branches contrast markedly with the winter sky; covered with hoar frost they are of a striking beauty and therefore it will be difficult to find a more attractive winter guest. Obviously a new tree should be sited so that it achieves the maximum effect.

As the tree grows older its crown becomes rounder and the stem thicker. The shoots are brittle and easily snap off.

The original species comes from North China and Korea. Though it thrives best in a moist soil its demands are minimal. Propagation presents no problems at all: any branch may be cut off and planted elsewhere; especially in a somewhat moist soil it will root easily and grow fast. Before planting in a dry place it is useful to water the ground thoroughly.

Like other willows the tree has catkins, but they are insignificant. However, the white back of the curling leaves, visible in the wind, is very decorative.

Salix sachalinensis 'Sekka'

SALIX SACHALINENSIS 'SEKKA'

A deviation that may occur in many kinds of plants is the so-called fasciation, which means that the stems become flattened and distorted. It can occur in all types of plants and is regarded as a freak.

The sturdy growing, always bushy, willow illustrated above comes from Japan. It has characteristic fasciation and is therefore interesting in all stages of its life. Even in young plants three, four or even more shoots fuse together and when their leaves are shed these stems are surprisingly decorative.

For flower arrangers S.s. 'Sekka' is favourite material, especially in modern arrangements, and also in dried form. In particular in the Japanese Ikebana style, these branches may contribute to interesting compositions. The plant stands cutting down to the ground in winter; in one season it will recover completely. Branches left on the shrub are richly covered with catkins in spring.

S.c. 'Sekka' is a strong grower and therefore especially suitable to the larger garden; it prefers moist soil. As with all willows, propagation is simple; even strong branches will root very easily.

Sambucus racemosa 'Plumosa Aurea'

SAMBUCUS (Elder)

The normal common elder has migrated from the Mediterranean countries all over Europe and is a common plant in the countryside. It is an attractive plant and the flowers, the berries, the pith and the branches are used for a number of purposes. In April—May they may be seen flowering with their flat creamy coloured umbels along the country roads and as it forms a good windbreak it is one of the shrubs chosen to protect the bulb fields in Cornwall.

A variety with finely cut leaves is S. racemosa, native to Europe. It is a broad, early flowering bush producing red berries. The yellow elder illustrated above is a variety with deeply cut leaves, which, when young, has a brownish tint that turns a golden yellow later in the season; they make the plant very conspicuous, even at a distance. This elder should not be planted in the full sun, but in a more shaded place, but even there its yellow leaves will brighten the garden.

Elders grow fast and high in any soil. As a consequence they are very useful as pioneer plants in a garden still waiting its final form. They accept any pruning, even cutting back to the ground; afterwards extra fine leaved shoots will come, however without flowers and berries in the first year. The berries have decorative value, and in the country they are used in a delicious jam or for wine making. Propagation is simple: in spring or autumn branches will easily root.

Skimmia reevesiana

SKIMMIA

A property which was hardly important in the past now makes Skimma of special interest: it can stand polluted air and may be used on factory sites and along motorways.

In autumn the flower buds for the next season appear and because of this colourful addition—S. foremanii has reddish-brown and S. reevesiana 'Rubella' attractive purple ones—the plants are a pleasing sight during the whole of winter.

In March or April the inconspicuous flowers appear in crowded terminal panicles, attracting many insects by their strong scent. S. foremanii is unisexual; the male flowers are finer but the female ones give fine red berries, often staying on the shrub until the following spring, as birds do not like them at all. A. reevesiana is a broad bush with narrow dark leaves and has male and female flowers on one plant. In the shade and on moist soil the latter are generally followed by crimson berries. Nurserymen often put several small plants into one pot and sell them as attractive pot plants for Christmas decoration.

The variety 'Rubella' has reddish leaf stalks and purple buds, but as all its flowers are male no berries may be expected.

In the garden skimmias remain rather low growing; a specimen of three feet is quite an exception. The soil should not be too dry and should contain some humus; in dry periods watering may be advisable as the many leaves evaporate a great deal of moisture. Skimmias prefer lime-free soil.

Skimmias should not be pruned; propagation is by cuttings.

Sorbus aucuparia

SORBUS (Mountain ash)

Though a mountain ash can be a tree of considerable height it deserves a place in this book as it may also be grown in shrub form; its growth makes it suitable for the smaller garden.

The common mountain ash—S. aucuparia—may be used as a pioneer plant to hold the soil or to protect a plot against sand carrying winds. It stands polluted air reasonably well—a valuable quality nowadays.

In the garden a mountain ash is an everlasting symphony of colours. First in spring the creamy-yellow flower heads attract many bees and when it is still full summer the colourful berries announce the autumn. The berries stay on the plant until October, providing a cheerful and colourful sight at a time that other plants have already lost their appeal. Even in places where other trees will barely survive, such as high in the mountains and on nearly treeless Iceland, mountain ash may be found.

Fine new varities, such as S.a. 'Edulis' and 'Sheerwater Seedling', often grow too fast for a small garden, but S. decora, with its fine dark green foliage and deep red fruits, is more suitable.

S. aria, the whitebeam, has several interesting forms, the greater part of them fast growing and therefore useful around a country house or as a background planting near a caravan or camping site; they fit nicely in a natural landscape.

It will be understandable that such a universal plant is not fastidious as to position or soil; it is very adaptable. Propagation of the species is by seeds.

Spiraea arguta　　　　　*S. vanhouttei*　　　　　*S. bumalda 'Anthony Waterer'*

SPIRAEA

The genus Spiraea includes species with an entirely different appearance, but all of them are bushy and are exceptionally free-flowering.

Already in May Spiraea arguta (Foam of May), with branches arching under the weight of umbels consisting of small white florets, is a marvellous sight. It may reach a height of about five feet and has a considerable spread; it can be used as a solitary specimen or in a loose hedge.

About the same time Spiraea vanhouttei displays even more abundant flowering, during which the whole shrub seems shrouded in a white mantle; this shrub grows to a height of about seven feet.

Of lower growth is the carmine-red flowering variety 'Anthony Waterer' of the species S. bumalda. Its flat flower heads will grow no higher than 30 inches; at the end of stiff branches they will unfold their florets from June till September.

All spiraeas are very hardy and contribute much to the colour of parks and gardens. They appreciate a sunny position and soil with much humus; in particular S. vanhouttei does not like shade.

The loose growth and arching branches of all spiraeas do not demand much pruning, but from time to time old branches may be removed.

Propagation is possible by cuttings, by dividing plants and by transplanting runners.

Symphoricarpos albus var. laviegatus

SYMPHORICARPOS (Snowberry)

This plant, which is native to the dry soils of North America, is very adaptable. It is extremely hardy and even survives where other shrubs might have given up a long time ago. It may be useful for planting on difficult embankments and to fill open places under trees.

The real snowberry is S. albus var. laviegatus, the white berries of which are illustrated above. They stay on the bare branches even in winter and are often used in Christmas and autumn flower arrangements.

S. orbiculatus is sometimes called coral berry on account of the shape of its purplish-rose berries. These also stay on the plant till after Christmas.

A great number of hybrids and selections are also worth noting. S. 'Turesson' is richly covered with oblong berries. 'Magic Berry' will reach about three feet and its purplish-red berries grow close together. 'Mother of Pearl, is a sturdy grower with large white berries and a pink glow, as the name implies. In particular S. 'White Hedge' is a good hedging plant. Its growth is erect and the white berries come in great numbers. S. chenaultii 'Erect' may be used for the same purpose.

All these shrubs make underground runners—a disadvantage in the small garden but an easy way for propagation. In addition, snowberries can be produced from cutting and plant divisions.

Syringa 'Souvenir de Louis Späth'　　*S. swegiflexa*

SYRINGA (Lilac)

After the first spring rush in the garden centres is over there is often a demand for lilacs. Earlier in the year customers, unless they know better, are not attracted by the small winter buds and it is not until the swollen flower buds are more obvious do they come to buy the plants—often a little too late in the season.

There are numerous lilac varieties, the greater part of them hybrids and often well established, but still among the best ones. Some excellent varieties are 'Decaisne' (sky blue single flowers—low growing), 'Hugo de Vries' (single purple flowers—high), 'Primrose' (light primrose yellow), 'Souvenir de Louis Spath' (single, deep purple, late flowering) and 'Madame Lemoine' (pure white, double).

The average lilac shrub grows to about twelve feet and the flowering period varies from year to year, as it is strongly dependant on the spring weather. At any rate it is between the first of May and the first of June. In general, the flowering lasts only for a short time but there are longer flowering species such as Syringa swegiflexa.

The sunnier the position the richer the flowering. Shrubs should be pruned regularly, preferably after flowering. A good way of pruning is to cut some branches during flowering for house decoration. Only young shoots will flower, and after pruning new shoots with buds will appear before winter. Suckers coming from the wild understock should be removed, if possible beneath the ground with the help of a spade, as they take the food from the main part of the shrub. Winter pruning should be only done on branches without flower buds. Propagation is by grafting.

Tamarix tetrandra

TAMARIX (Tamarisk)

In the average garden a tamarisk is hard to combine with other plants and therefore it is most satisfactory as a solitary specimen on a lawn, near a pond, or contrasting with a dark hedge.

It is a graceful plant with small scale-like leaves, at first sight like a conifer. The arching branches make it extremely elegant and the flowers, long pink feathery heads, cover the shrub like a veil.

T. tetrandra, the earliest one, unfolds its flowers before the leaves. T. pentandra does not flower before August–September; its flowers are darker pink, and with the variety 'Rubra' even carmine-red.

Early flowering species develop their flowers on the old branches, the others on young shoots. This should be taken into account when pruning: the former should be pruned immediately after flowering, the latter late in winter, in order to make the plant more compact and to promote branching.

Old shrubs should not be pruned except when they grow too high or when branches flower only poorly.

They are resistant to strong winds and are amongst the best shrubs for planting in exposed sites near the coast, however, a sheltered position in a soil with humus will promote the best growth and beauty of a tamarisk. Some peat moss in the planting hole is helpful. Propagation is by cuttings.

Taxodium distichum

TAXODIUM DISTICHUM (Swamp cypress)

This fine, deciduous conifer comes from the swamps in the eastern United States where it has characteristic "knee"-like roots, presumably to carry air to the submerged roots. In the German city of Dortmund a specimen has thrived in deep water for more than twelve years and this may prove that a soil is never too wet for this tree.

The swamp cypress fits well in the European landscape and often grows better here than in its native land, from which it came about 300 years ago. In summer it is covered with fine thin leaves and in autumn, when the foliage turns to a rich brown, the needles are shed together with the secondary branchlets, giving the tree a very bare appearance in winter. The growth is slow and it takes over a quarter of a century before any "knees" are formed.

The swamp cypress appreciates a moist soil but makes no other demands. In a storm it will survive where other trees fall. As the tree sheds its lower branches naturally it does not need pruning. Propagation is by seeds.

Taxus baccata

T. b. 'Fastigiata'

TAXUS (Yew)

In Western Europe the number of wild conifers is limited, but the yew is one of them. It is a pity that the wild species are getting scarce, though it is said that they may reach an age of more than a thousand years. The yew is the best of all evergreens for hedge making and particularly for topiary work. In our gardens the cultivated yews are numerous. Little flowers are followed by the appearance of red fleshy fruits with poisonous seeds. The leaves are also poisonous, so the yew should not be planted where it can be eaten by animals, such as cattle and horses.

There are many different forms. The illustrated T. baccata 'Fastigiata' starts as a pillar and develops to a vase shape, just as its yellow varieties. A recommended kind for hedging is the new erect-growing 'Raket'. The spreading 'Repandens', which branches horizontally, may be used in low plantings and as a ground cover. Well known is T. cuspidata, a small tree in Japan, its country of origin, and used as a hedge-forming shrub in this part of the world. A spreading variety is T. cuspidata 'Nana' with short broad leaves; from a cross between T. baccata and T. cuspidata came the new T. media. A good selection from America is T.m. 'Hicksii', a wide column with dark green foliage, also a good hedging plant but easily falling apart under a burden of snow.

All these varieties grow in any reasonable garden soil, in the shade as well as in the sun provided the soil is not too moist. Pruning should be done in summer. T. baccata can even be clipped and trained to various forms. This species is propagated by seeds, the other by cuttings.

Thuja occidentalis 'Pyramidalis Compacta'   *T. o. 'Rheingold'*

THUJA (Arbor-vitae)

This genus includes an important group of conifers used in many gardens. Thuja occidentalis, the white cedar of Canada, was brought to Europe in the second half of the 16th century. In particular the illustrated variety, T.o. 'Pyramidalis Compacta'—the name reveals its compact conical shape—and T.o. 'Rosenthalii', with a darker foliage and a slower growth, are useful hedging plants. They stand clipping very well, but not in the same way as with privet hedges: in summer they should be trimmed with sharp shears, as a branch cut too deeply will never sprout again. Solitary plants never need pruning; their natural shape is a beautiful cone.

Like many conifers, thujas are variable plants; this has enabled nurserymen to make fine selections. Many of them are great assets to the rockery, such as T.o. 'Globosa' which is a small bright green globe. 'Little Gem' is somewhat flatter and very hardy. The yellow 'Rheingold' may be globe- or cone-shaped and turns to a darker shade in winter. A good novelty suitable for the small garden is 'Tiny Tim'; this variety may be used in window-boxes or containers, mixed with annuals in summer.

Thuja grown as hedging plants should be planted about 2 ft. apart and they will make a good hedge within a few years. To promote spreading the tops are pruned. The soil is not important but a light position is favourable, the shrubs getting thin in the shade. They stand wind better than many other conifers.

Varieties can be propagated by cuttings, the species by seeds.

Vaccinium vitis-idaea

VACCINIUM VITIS-IDAEA (Cowberry)

This small shrub is native to the high woods and moors of northern Europe. The branches are covered with soft hairs and can spread until the diameter of the plant is about 40 inches. Its leaves are glossy dark green and obovate with slightly curled edges. In May–June racemes of about one inch appear; they are covered with near white or pale pink florets which can be seen on close observation.

Later large numbers of small berries will appear and stay on the plant part of the winter. It is for this reason that cowberries make ideal pot plants.

In the garden it is a good ground cover, and can be grown in rockeries and heather gardens. The plant stands half-shade and in a reasonably moist soil it will spread nicely, making rootrunners in the meantime. If the plant, by growing higher, loses its ground-hugging characteristics the tops can be cut off with pruning shears. The fruits, which ripen in August, are edible; in the past they were used as a medicine, for instance as a cure for rheumatism.

Propagation is simple. The plants can be divided easily and rooted runners can be planted elsewhere. In addition they can be produced from seed without difficulty.

A related plant is the swamp—or high-bush blueberry—V. corymbosum. Several varieties with large fruits are grown for commercial purposes and may be of interest to fruit growing gardeners. There are also a great many other species of vaccinium including whortleberries, bilberries, and cranberries.

Viburnum opulus 'Roseum'   *V. rhytidophyllum*

VIBURNUM

Viburnum is a genus of great variation as to the shape of the leaves, growing and flowering habits; it includes evergreen as well as deciduous plants.

Well known is the native Guelder rose—V. opulus—of which the variety 'Roseum' is a beautiful garden plant, though it may exceed 12 feet in height. The older name, 'Sterile', indicates that the plant never bears fruits, contrary to the species which produce trans-lucent red ovoid berries in autumn. In June the branches, bearing bright green foliage, are laden with flowering heads like snowballs, first greenish then white and pinkish at the end of the season. V. carlesii is a round shrub not higher than five feet, with fine fragrant heads of flowers often blossoming in March. A hybrid of the species is V. carl-cephalum with pink, later white, fragrant flowers coming from brown buds unfolding somewhat later than those on V. carlesii; its growth is stronger.

From China came the remarkable C. rhytidophyllum with wrinkled lanceolate leaves, the upper surface glossy green and the underside covered by grey or buff felt-like hairs. Being evergreen this viburnum makes a decorative garden plant throughout the year. Its white flower heads are formed in autumn and persist throughout the winter, opening from April to June. Planted several together in a group, they will bear lots of red berries, turning black later in the season. The erect growing branches make the plant suitable to smaller gardens. This species is an excellent plant for a chalky soil.

Pruning can be limited to removing of bothersome branches. Propagation is by cuttings and grafting.

Vinca minor

VINCA (Periwinkle)

The periwinkle belongs to a genus containing hardy and non-hardy plants, some of them deciduous and others evergreen. Among them are mat-forming plants, perennials and greenhouse plants—really an amazing variation.

Vinca major—the greater periwinkle—is an interesting plant now naturalised in western Europe, including Britain, and is a spreading sub-shrub with glossy, ovate, mid to dark green leaves. In the course of the centuries it moved slowly from its original native region in western Asia and eastern Europe to western Europe, and with the tendency to more natural gardens it deserves our attention more than ever.

V. major may reach a height of 12 inches and a spread of four feet. It has large blue flowers, contrasting nicely with the green foliage; the flowering period is from April to June and with a second flowering in September/October there are nearly always some flowers on the plant during summer.

Less well known and not quite so hardy is the lesser periwinkle—V. minor—with many named varieties. It is of a creeping habit and thus seldom grows higher than eight inches. The blue or white flowers appear in March and generally continue until October.

The periwinkles do not need sunshine and grow even in deep shade; fallen leaves do no damage to them.

Propagation is by division.

Weigela 'Eva Rathke'   *Weigela florida 'Nana Variegata'*

WEIGELA

The name Weigela may create some confusion, as although for years it has been well known under that name, it was for a short time named Diervilla.

There are important improvements in the choice of varieties and W. 'Eva Rathke', illustrated above, has been surpassed by the novelty 'Eva Supreme', which will be available from garden centres and nurserymen in the near future, but it takes a long time before older varieties disappear.

Weigelas, originating from Japan, generally flower in early summer, but by making the correct choice of varieties the flowering period may last about ten weeks.

The colours range between red and pink, for example 'Newport Red' is dark red and 'Rosabella' is pink with a bright red edge, being the lightest variety. W. florida 'Nana Variegata', illustrated above, may be chosen on account of its variegated leaves.

All varieties are satisfied with a reasonable garden soil and need some years to reach full size, however they will do best in the sun and on a well-manured soil.

Pruning should be restricted to cutting back old branches that spoil the shape of the shrub or restrict the growth of the shoots in the centre. Old shoots that have flowered can be cut back after flowering. Propagation is by cuttings.

WISTERIA SINENSIS (Chinese wisteria)

In the experimental garden in Boskoop, Holland, the largest nursery centre in the world, experts have discovered remarkable things about Wisteria. They already knew that there was a tremendous difference in the number of flowers and in the length of the flowering period of plants sold under the name W. sinensis. By selecting the best new varieties have been bred. In future these will find their way to the nurseries throughout the whole world and as a consequence buyers may feel sure that they are buying plants with the best flowering chances.

In May the showy 8–12 inches long racemes of fragrant mauve flowers appear on the bare branches. Later leaves, consisting of up to eleven leaflets, will appear, hiding a second, less prolific, flowering in summer.

The position of the plant is of great importance to the flowering. On the east side of a house, protected against northern winds where the plant enjoys the cool morning sun but is not affected by the stronger sunrays of the afternoon, numerous flowers may appear. An interesting combination is to grow a wisteria together with a laburnum as the plants flower at the same time. The limited growth of the wisteria will not hurt the host plant.

As to the soil, it is important that it contains no lime. Pruning should be done just above the new flower buds as growth begins in early spring. Propagation by layering is simple: lower vines touching the soil will be rooted after a year and can be transplanted elsewhere. Grafting on its own roots and taking cuttings are also practicable.

INDICES AND SUMMARIES

1. Average Flowering Periods
(Conifers and other plants which owe their decorative value solely to foliage, fruits or other qualities, are not listed).
(The periods stated are average as the difference in flowering, especially in spring, might be four weeks between the southern and the northern part of the British Isles.)

January
Cornus mas
Erica carnea
Hamamelis japonica
Hamamelis mollis
Jasminum nudiflorum

February
Cornus mas
Corylus
Daphne mezereum
Erica carnea
Hamamelis japonica
Hamamelis mollis
Jasminum nudiflorum
Rhododendron praecox
Vinca

March
Chaenomeles
Cornus mas
Corylopsis
Corylus
Daphne mezereum
Erica carnea
Hamamelis japonica
Hamamelis mollis
Jasminum nudiflorum
Magnolia stellata
Pachysandra terminalis
Pieris floribunda
Pieris japonica
Prunus triloba
Rhododendron praecox
Salix
Skimmia
Vinca

April
Amelanchier
Chaenomeles
Cornus mas
Corylopsis
Cytisus praecox
Erica carnea

(*April continued*)
Forsythia
Jasminum nudiflorum
Magnolia stellata
Magnolia liliflora
Mahonia aquifolium
Malus
Pachysandra terminalis
Pieris floribunda
Pieris japonica
Prunus subhirtella
Prunus triloba
Rhododendron praecox
Ribes
Salix
Sambucus racemosa
Skimmia
Spiraea arguta
Viburnum carlesii
Viburnum carlcephalum
Vinca
Wisteria

May
Amelanchier
Azalea
Berberis
Callicarpa
Caragana arborescens
Clematis (large and small flowering)
Cornus alba
Cornus florida
Cornus kousa
Cotoneaster
Crataegus
Cytisus praecox
Cytisus scoparius
Deutzia gracilis
Enkianthus
Forsythia
Kalmia
Kerria japonica
Kolkwitzia amabilis
Laburnum
Lonicera tatarica

140

(*May continued*)
Lonicera tellmaniana
Magnolia liliflora
Mahonia aquifolium
Malus
Pernettya mucronata
Philadelphus coronarius
Pieris floribunda
Pieris japonica
Prunus laurocerasus
Prunus subhirtella
Pyracantha
Ribes
Rosa
Sambucus racemosa
Skimmia
Sorbus aria
Sorbus aucuparia
Spiraea arguta
Spiraea vanhouttei
Syringa vulgaris
Tamarix tetrandra
Viburnum carlesii
Viburnum carlcephalum
Viburnum rhytidophyllum
Weigela
Wisteria

June
Aesculus parviflora
Ailanthus altissima
Aristolochia durior
Celastrus scandens
Clematis (large flowering)
Colutea aborescens
Cornus alba
Cornus kousa
Cotinus coggygria
Cotoneaster
Crataegus
Cytisus scoparlus
Deutzia gracilis
Deutzia kalmiaeflora
Deutzia hybr. 'Mont Rose'
Eleagnus angustifolia
Erica cinerea
Genista tinctoria
Gleditsia
Hydrangea petiolaris
Hypericum
Kalmia
Kerria japonica
Kolkwitzia amabilis
Laburnum

(*June continued*)
Ligustrum vulgare
Lonicera caprifolium
Lonicera periclymenum
Lonicera tatarica
Lonicera tellmaniana
Magnolia liliflora
Malus
Osmanthus ilicifolius
Passiflora
Pernettya mucronata
Philadelphus coronarius
Potentilla fruticosa
Rhododendron
Rhus typhina
Robinia hispida
Rosa
Spiraea bumalda
Spiraea vanhouttei
Symphoricarpos
Syringa swegiflexa
Syringa vulgaris
Vaccinium vitis-idaea
Viburnum carlcephalum
Viburnum rhytidophyllum
Weigela
Wisteris

July
Aesculus parviflora
Ailanthus altissima
Aristolochia durior
Buddleia davidii
Calluna vulgaris
Campsis radicans
Ceanothus 'Gloire de Versailles'
Clematis (large flowering)
Colutea arborescens
Cotinus coggygria
Deutzia hybr. 'Mont Rose'
Eleagnus angustifolia
Erica cinerea
Gaultheria procumbens
Genista tinctoria
Gleditsia
Hibiscus syriacus
Hydrangea arborescens
Hydrangea paniculata
Hydrangea paniculata 'Grandiflora'
Hydrangea petiolaris
Hypericum
Ligustrum ovalifolium
Ligustrum vulgare
Lonicera caprifolium

(*July continued*)
Lonicera periclymenum
Lonicera tatarica
Osmanthus ilicifolius
Passiflora
Polygonum
Potentilla fruticosa
Rhus typhina
Rosa
Sambucus nigra
Spiraea bumalda
Symphoricarpos orbiculatus
Syringa swegiflexa

August
Aesculus parviflora
Aralia alata
Buddleia davidii
Calluna vulgaris
Campsis radicans
Ceanothus 'Gloire de Versailles'
Clematis (large flowering)
Colutea arborescens
Erica cinerea
Gaultheria procumbens
Genista tinctoria
Hibiscus syriacus
Hydrangea arborescens
Hydrangea paniculata
Hydrangea paniculata 'Grandiflora'
Hydrangea petiolaris
Hypericum
Ligustrum ovalifolium
Lonicera periclymenum
Osmanthus ilicifolius
Passiflora
Polygonum
Potentilla fruticosa
Rosa
Tamarix pentandra

September
Buddleia davidii
Calluna vulgaris
Campsis radicans
Ceanothus 'Gloire de Versailles'
Clematis (large flowering)
Colutea aborescens
Hedera helix
Hibiscus syriacus
Hydrandea arborescens
Hydrangea paniculata
Hydrangea paniculata 'Grandiflora'
Hypericum
Passiflora
Polygonum
Potentilla fruticosa
Robinia hispida
Rosa
Tamarix pentandra

October
Calluna vulgaris
Ceanothus 'Gloire de Versailles'
Clematis (large flowering)
Colutea arborescens
Hedera helix
Polygonum
Potentilla fruticosa
Rosa

November
Calluna vulgaris
Hedera helix
Jasminum nudiflorum

December
Erica carnea
Hamamelis mollis
Jasminum nudiflorum

142

2. Plants Suitable for a Sunny Position

(If no species or varieties are mentioned all members of the genus described in this book are suitable.)

Abies
Acer japonica
Acer negundo
Ailanthus
Amelanchier
Berberis
Buddleia
Buxus
Callicarpa
Calluna
Campsis
Caragana
Ceanothus
Cedrus
Chamaecyparis
Chaenomeles
Clematis
Colutea
Cornus
Corylopsis
Corylus
Cotinus
Cotoneaster
Crataegus
Cytisus

Eleagnus
Erica
Euonymus
Forsythia
Gaultheria
Genista
Ginkgo
Gleditsia
Hamamelis japonica
Hibiscus
Hippophae
Hypericum
Ilex crenata
Ilex verticillata
Jasminum
Juniperus
Kerria
Kolkwitzia
Laburnum
Ligustrum
Liquidambar
Lonicera
Magnolia
Mahonia
Malus

Metasequoia
Philadelphus
Picea
Pinus
Potentilla
Prunus (P. laurocerasus excepted)
Pyracantha
Rhus
Ribes
Robinia
Rosa
Salix
Sambucus
Sorbus
Spiraea
Symphoricarpos
Syringa
Tamarix
Taxodium
Thuja
Viburnum
Weigela

---

3. Plants Suitable for Half Shade

(If no species or varieties are mentioned all members of the genus described in this book are suitable.)

Acer negundo
Acer palmatum
Amelanchier
Berberis
Buxus
Callicarpa
Calluna
Caragana
Chaenomeles
Chamaecyparis
Clematis
Colutea
Cornus alba
Cornus florida
Cornus stolonifera
  'Flaviramea'
Corylopsis
Cotoneaster
Crataegus
Cryptomeria
Daphne
Deutzia

Enkianthus
Erica
Euonymus
Forsythia
Hamamelis
Hedera
Hydrangea
Hypericum
Ilex
Jasminum
Juniperus
Kalmia
Kerria
Kolkwitzia
Laburnum
Ligustrum
Lonicera
Magnolia
Mahonia
Pachysandra
Parthenocissus
Pernettya

Philadelphus
Picea omorika
Picea pungens
Pieris
Polygonum
Prunus cerasifera
Prunus laurocerasus
Pyracantha
Rhododendron
Rhus
Ribes
Robinia
Sambucus
Skimmia
Sorbus
Spiraea
Symphoricarpos
Syringa vulgaris
Taxodium
Taxus
Vinca minor
Wisteria

4. Plants Suitable for a Shady Position

(If no species or varieties are mentioned all members of the genus described in this book are suitable.)

Aesculus
Amelanchier
Berberis buxifolia 'Nana'
Buxus
Callicarpa
Chamaecyparis obtusa
Clematis
Cornus alba
Corylus
Cotoneaster watereri
Crataegus monogyna
Daphne
Enkianthus
Gaultheria

Hedera
Hydrangea
Hypericum
Ilex aquifolium
Kalmia angustifolia
   'Rubra'
Kerria
Kolkwitzia
Ligustrum ovalifolium
Ligustrum vulgare
Lonicera pileata
Lonicera tatarica
Pachysandra
Pernettya

Pieris
Prunus laurocerasus
Pyracantha
Rhododendron
Ribes
Sambucus nigra
Skimmia
Sorbus aucuparia
Spiraea arguta
Spiraea vanhouttei
Taxus
Viburnum
Vinca minor

5. Plants with a Reasonable Resistance to Air Pollution

(If no species or varieties are mentioned all members of the genus described in this book are suitable.)

Acer negundo
Ailanthus
Berberis buxifolia 'Nana'
Buddleia
Buxus
Calluna
Cedrus atlantica 'Glauca'
Chaenomeles
Chamaecyparis
Cornus alba
Corylus
Cotoneaster
Crataegus monogyna
Eleagnus
Erica
Euonymus alata
Euonymus radicans
Forsythia

Gaultheria
Ginkgo
Gleditsia
Hamamelis japonica
Hedera
Hydrangea paniculata
   'Grandiflora'
Hypericum
Ilex aquifolium
Ilex crenata
Jasminum
Juniperus sabina
   'Tamariscifolia'
Kalmia
Kerria
Ligustrum vulgare
Liquidambar
Lonicera pileata

Lonicera tatarica
Magnolia liliflora 'Nigra'
Mahonia
Metasequoia
Pachysandra
Parthenocissus
Picea omorika
Picea pungens
Pieris
Philadelphus
Pinus mugo
Pinus pumila
Prunus laurocerasus
Pyracantha
Rhododendron praecox
Sambucus
Skimmia
Symphoricarpos

6. Plants Tolerating Sea Winds

(w = green in winter.)

Crataegus monogyna
Eleagnus angustifolia
Eleagnus ebbingei (w)
Erica carnea
(many, but not all, varieties) (w)

Euonymus europaea
Hippophae rhamnoides
Ligustrum vulgare
Potentilla fruticosa

Rosa rugosa
Sambucus nigra
Sorbus aria
Tamarix

7. Plants that do well in Limy or Chalky Soil

Berberis (some species and varieties)
Buddleia
Buxus sempervirens
Chaenomeles (some varieties)
Colutea
Corylus
Cotinus
Cotoneaster (some varieties)
Crataegus (some varieties)
Eleagnus (some varieties)
Erica carnea (some varieties)
Euonymus

Hippophae
Laburnum watereri 'Vossii'
Ligustrum vulgare
Philadelphus (many varieties)
Prunus (some varieties)
Pyracantha (some varieties)
Rhus typhina
Sorbus aria
Symphoricarpos (a few varieties)
Syringa vulgaris
Viburnum opulus

8. Plants that do well in Humus-containing Soils

Acer palmatum (many varieties)
Azalea
Berberis thunbergii
Callicarpa
Calluna vulgaris (many varieties)
Cornus florida
Cornus stolonifera 'Flaviramea'
Cotoneaster sal. var. floccosa
Enkianthus
Erica (most variotics)
Hamamelis (a few varieties)

Hydrangea (a few varieties)
Hypericum (a few varieties)
Ilex aquifolium (many varieties)
Ilex crenata (a few varieties)
Lonicera (some varieties)
Magnolia (a few varieties)
Pieris
Potentilla (many varieties)
Rhododendron (most varieties)
Viburnum (a few varieties)
Weigela (many varieties)

(In case of doubt your supplier will gladly advise)

9. Hedging Plants

Berberis thunbergii (some varieties)
Buxus sempervirens
Crataegus monogyna
Ilex (many species)
Ligustrum (many species)
Lonicera pileata

Potentilla fruticosa 'Arbuscula'
Potentilla fruticosa 'Maanelys'
Prunus laurocerasus 'Reynvaanii'
Spiraea bumalda 'Anthony Waterer'
Spiraea vanhouttei
Symphoricarpos

10. Climbing Plants

Campsis
Celastrus
Clematis (many varieties)
Hedera helix
Hydrangea petiolaris
Jasminum

Lonicera (some species)
Parthenocissus
Polygonum
Pyracantha (some varieties)
Rosa (ramblers)
Wisteria

11. Evergreen Groundcover

Calluna (some varieties)
Cotoneaster dammeri
Cotoneaster salicifolia
Erica carnea (many varieties)
Hedera helix

Hypericum calycinum
Pachysandra
Potentilla fruticosa 'Arbuscula'
Vinca major
Vinca minor

12. Plants with Attractive Fruits

Amelanchier
Aucuba
Berberis (most of the species)
Callicarpa
Celastrus
Chaenomeles
Cornus
Cotoneaster
Crataegus
Daphne (the berries are poisonous)
Euonymus (not all of them)
Gaultheria
Hedera helix 'Arborescens'
Hippophae

Ilex aquifolium
Ilex verticillata
Mahonia
Malus (not all species)
Pernettya
Pyracantha
Rhus
Rosa (many species)
Skimmia
Sorbus
Symphoricarpos
Vaccinium corymbosum
Vaccinium vitis-idaea
Viburnum (many species)

13. Plants with Colourful Foliage

(w = green in winter.)

Acer negundo
Acer palmatum
Aucuba (w)
Berberis thunbergii 'Atropurpurea'
Calluna vulgaris (variegated varieties) (w)
Cornus alba
Corylus maxima 'Purpurea'

Cotinus coggygria 'Royal Purple'
Gleditsia
Ilex aquifolium (gold and silver variegated) (w)
Ilex crenata 'Golden Gem'
Ligustrum ovalifolium 'Aureum'
Sambucus racemosa 'Plumosa Aurea'
Weigela florida 'Nana Variegata'

14. Plants with Autumn Colours

Acer palmatum
Amelanchier
Berberis thunbergii
Cotinus coggygria 'Royal Purple'
Cotoneaster horizontalis 'Robusta'
Euonymus alata

Euonymus europaea
Gleditsia
Liquidambar
Parthenocissus tricuspidata 'Veitchii'
Rhus typhina

15. Plants with Colourful Bark

Cornus alba 'Kesselringii'
Cornus stolonifera 'Flaviramea'
Kerria japonica

146

ALPHABETICAL LIST
OF DESCRIBED PLANTS

INDEX